HEALTHY EATING FOR YOUR
BABY & TODDLER

RENÉE ELLIOTT

HEALTHY EATING FOR YOUR
BABY & TODDLER

Delicious Recipes Right from the Start

DUNCAN BAIRD PUBLISHERS

LONDON

I dedicate this book to the family I was born into and the family I gave birth to.

HEALTHY EATING FOR YOUR BABY & TODDLER
Renée Elliott

Distributed in the USA and Canada by
Sterling Publishing Co., Inc.
387 Park Avenue South
New York, NY 10016-8810

First published in the UK and USA in 2010 by
Duncan Baird Publishers Ltd
Sixth Floor, Castle House
75–76 Wells Street
London W1T 3QH

Managing Editor: Grace Cheetham
Editor: Nicole Bator
Managing Designer: Manisha Patel
Designer: Luana Gobbo
Commissioned photography: Simon Smith
Food Stylist: Mari Mererid Williams
Prop Stylist: Wei Tang

Library of Congress Cataloging-in-Publication Data

Elliott, Renée J.
  Healthy eating for your baby & toddler : delicious recipes right from the start / Renée Elliot.
      p. cm.
  Includes index.
  ISBN 978-1-84483-903-2
  1. Infants--Nutrition. 2. Toddlers--Nutrition. 3. Natural foods. I. Title.
  RJ216.E45 2010
  641.5'6222--dc22
                    2009052495

ISBN: 978-1-84483-903-2

10 9 8 7 6 5 4 3 2 1

Typeset in Frutiger, Univers, Clarendon and Berranger Hand
Color reproduction by Scanhouse, Malaysia
Printed in Thailand by Imago

For information about custom editions, special sales, premium and corporate purchases, please contact Sterling Special Sales Department at 800-805-5489 or specialsales@sterlingpub.com.

Publisher's note
While every care has been taken in compiling the recipes for this book, Duncan Baird Publishers, or any other persons who have been involved in working on this publication, cannot accept responsibility for any errors or omissions, inadvertent or not, that may be found in the recipes or text, nor for any problems that may arise as a result of preparing one of these recipes. If you are pregnant or breastfeeding or have any special dietary requirements or medical conditions, it is advisable to consult a medical professional before following any of the recipes contained in this book.

Notes on the recipes
Unless otherwise stated:
Use organic ingredients
Use extra-large eggs, and medium fruit and vegetables
Use fresh ingredients, including herbs
1 tsp. = 5ml   1 tbsp. = 15ml   1 cup = 240ml

Symbols are used to identify even small amounts of an ingredient, such as the seeds symbol for sesame oil. Dairy foods in this book can include cow, goat, or sheep milk. The vegetarian symbol is given to recipes using cheese; please check the manufacturer's labeling before purchase to ensure cheeses are vegetarian. Ensure that only the relevantly identified foods are given to anyone with a food allergy or intolerance.

Acknowledgments
Huge thanks, hugs, and kisses to my husband Brian and my kids for eating my food and being so patient; my Mom for her recipes; Julia for her total support; Nathalie for caring for my children; Allison for helping out without being asked; Veronica for her encouragement; Molly for tuna pie and shrimp bake; and Maggie for the knife. Thank you to Borra, Grace, Luana, and Nicole. Without you there simply wouldn't be a book. And to Suzannah Olivier, whose book *What Should I Feed My Baby?* inspired me when I was a new mother.

contents

KEY TO SYMBOLS

 Vegetarian: Contains no meat, poultry, game, fish, shellfish, or animal by-products.

 Wheat-free: Contains no wheat, wheat flour, or wheat products.

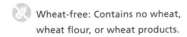 Gluten-free: Contains no gluten-based grains or products, including wheat, barley, rye, oat, spelt, and Kamut.

 Dairy-free: Contains no dairy products, including milk, cheese, yogurt, kefir, or butter.

 Egg-free: Contains no eggs or egg products.

 Nut-free: Contains no nuts (almonds, Brazil nuts, cashew nuts, chestnuts, coconut, hazelnuts, macadamia nuts, peanuts, pecans, pine nuts, pistachio nuts, and walnuts) or nut oils.

 Seed-free: Contains no seeds (flax, hemp, pumpkin, safflower, sesame, and sunflower) or seed oils.

foreword

I am the jars of baby food my mom fed me as an infant. I am the endless pots of Creole stew she stirred on the stove. I am my mom chopping onions at the counter. My mom taking yet another batch of cookies out of the oven. My dad teaching us how to tie up the tomato plants and when to pick the ripe summer squash. My brother and sisters standing in the slanting fall sun, crunching cucumbers sprinkled with salt.

I am the university student who studied health and aging. The adventurer who followed her heart and came to England. The employee who realized she had to love and believe in what she did. I am the entrepreneur who started Planet Organic. And, I am the mother who learned to cook all over again. I am not, however, a trained chef. I, like you, simply have to feed my family.

Growing up, the kitchen table was where we sat together to share food; where I watched my mom roll out endless pastry dough to make endless pies; and where we chatted as a family over morning coffee. Food is important to me and, as I have grown up and had my own children, it has become even more important.

I was running Planet Organic when I had my daughter Jessica, and between caring for her and working, I had no time at all. Then I had Nicholas, continued working and then had Cassandra. With three children, putting meals together had to be easier than ever.

Like everyone else, I want convenience in my life. All too often, however, convenience comes at the expense of health, whether through eating processed foods or ready meals, or swallowing a pill to feel better when we are sick. Twenty years ago I realized there was a better way to eat, live, and age. I started to question the majority of food that was for sale in the supermarkets. I learned about organic foods, nutrition, and alternative therapies, such as homeopathy and acupuncture, and I decided that I wasn't willing to take convenience at the expense of my, or my children's, health.

But even I, who love food and cooking, don't want to be—and can't be—in the kitchen all day. So this book is about making things easy. It's about quick, uncomplicated food, like boiling some pasta or opening a tin of sardines, and it's also about slow-cooked, rich autumn stews and long-rise bread. Above all, it's about giving your baby the best, healthiest start in life and creating healthy habits that will last a lifetime.

It is, however, no ordinary cookbook. It combines my own knowledge with the knowledge I have gained from other experts, ideas that make sense to me, and methods that worked with my kids. It will change the way you eat and think about food. You'll see many familiar ingredients here, alongside many that will probably be new to you. Don't worry. You'll soon understand exactly what kombu, kefir, and miso are, and why I think these "unusual" foods are so important for your child.

My approach might present for you a completely different way of eating and cooking—one that will create an entirely new relationship between you and your food. I'm not saying that this is the only way to wean and feed your baby. I'm saying, try this. I think it's the best way. But don't be too rigid; there aren't a lot of definite rights and wrongs. Many ideas and methods for babies have not yet been proven, and new research emerges all the time. So, I say, take advice—and then listen to your intuition.

Understanding the choices you have when feeding your child is so important, especially if you don't know a lot about food, your body, or how to create good health through good nutrition. Eating healthily is vital, and eating organic is the best thing for you. Don't worry about what you cooked or ate in the past; try something new. Focus on today. Be happy you have this book in your hands now. Be grateful that you know more now or are willing to explore and learn.

I can't emphasize enough how important it is to make changes slowly so it isn't stressful and so you incorporate them into your life going forward. Introduce a few new good foods and get rid of a few old bad habits each month. If you do too much too quickly, you won't persevere. Take it slowly and make these changes to last a lifetime. If you have just become pregnant, you can start making changes to your family's diet now or any time over the months until your baby is born. If your newborn is ready to wean, you can start now. Anyone can do this.

I can't wait for you to find your own favorites in these pages. For you to try different whole grains, different flavors, different techniques. To think about adding extra nutrition when you can. To realize that every bite counts and to waste fewer of them than you are now—but to still make a treat of organic chocolate every now and then. To discover the favorite recipes your child will want you to cook again and again. To find the way to health and vitality.

Renée Elliott

introduction

For most of us, having children delivers a massive jolt to our sense of priorities. I'm no exception. I had built my career and lifestyle around my love of food and interest in health, but it all took on an entirely new significance when I had my children and realized I was completely responsible for their nutrition and well-being. Suddenly, what had been interesting became incredibly important. I knew that what I taught my children about food when they were young would be with them for a lifetime. Cooking delicious, homemade food became a huge priority for me, as well as an immense pleasure. If you want to give your child—and yourself—a healthier, more satisfying way of eating, this book is for you.

I know from my own experience that being a new mother, particularly a first-time mother, is hard. Your life has been turned on its head, you might not be sleeping much, you never seem to have enough time to do everything you have to do—and this adorable but demanding little person is with you all the time. I now have three young children and, though I like to think I'm doing the best feeding the third, I learned the most with the first, because we had so much time together, and she was the only one seeking my attention.

With each new addition to our family, I adapted what I had learned. This book has evolved from that experience. It's about ease, variety, and taste and, above all, about optimizing nutrition and health for your baby and yourself, not only now but for the rest of your lives. Whether you are just learning to cook with this book and this baby or you are trying to figure out how to introduce organic, wholesome, homemade food into your busy life, now is your opportunity to get started. It won't be long before you'll be off and running: swapping ingredients, adding a little of this and a little of that, and changing recipes to meet your child's growing tastes and health needs.

Why is Health so Important?

Some people worry about giving their child a good education or getting him to excel at sports or a musical instrument, but for me the most important thing is health. You can have the brightest, most-gifted, most well-educated child, but without good health, he won't go far. With good health, he can achieve his dreams and fulfil his potential. And it's easier to be happy when you're healthy.

I'm not just talking about your child being well today or when he's a teenager. This is about creating health and healthy habits to last a lifetime, without so many of the diseases that affect people in our society. Being well now is also about aging well—for your child and for yourself, so you can enjoy him and his children for many years to come.

Unfortunately, you can eat bad food for years and feel okay—but you can be slowly creating unease in your body that becomes disease as you age. Heart disease, liver disease, and diabetes, all of which have been linked to diet, take years to develop.

There's so much in our world that is damaging, and which we can control very little, or not at all. Polluted air, chemically treated water, formaldehyde-laced carpets and curtains, noxious cleaning materials used in the exaggerated war on germs and, of course, stress all take their toll on the body. While you can't do that much about those things, you can control what your family eats. What you put in your child's mouth are the only ingredients that his body has to grow and to nurture and repair itself.

Good Food versus Bad Food

Think about the ingredients you give your body every day. Don't assume a food is good for you simply because it's allowed to be sold. The truth is many farmers, manufacturers, and retailers are not concerned about your health. They're running a business. Some sell good food; some sell bad. How can you tell the difference?

Highly processed, refined products like store-bought cakes, breads, doughnuts, sausages, fast food, carbonated drinks, and candies belong to the bad-food category. The length of the ingredients list is a strong clue as to whether a food is good or bad. If the list is long, particularly with words you don't understand, chances are it's a food you and your child would be better off without. My motto is: if you don't know what it is, don't put it into your body. If your granny wouldn't cook with it, forget it.

Basic ingredients to avoid are hydrogenated fats, monosodium glutamate (MSG), and artificial flavorings and colorings, additives, and preservatives. Hydrogenated fats are laden with trans fats, which are highly processed fats that the human body cannot process. These fats tend to congregate at fatty sites in the body and are difficult to excrete. They're used because they are cheap, easy to work with, and extend a food's shelf life. Artificial preservatives also make bad, cheap food last longer than it should, and artificial flavors, colors, and additives make it taste and look better. A chocolate chip cookie made with hydrogenated fat and artificial ingredients can sit on the supermarket shelf for months, losing what little nutritional value it has as it ages. The same cookie made with butter and natural ingredients will go out of date more quickly because its ingredients are perishable. You can choose to eat the fresh cookie or the old cookie. It's up to you. But who wants to eat old food? I don't.

Good food comes directly from nature: fruit, vegetables, grains, nuts, seeds, dairy, fish, and meat. It does not contain chemicals or lots of additives. Good food is organic food. Some processed foods, including cookies and snacks, can be good, but when you read the label, you should understand the ingredients list—and the shorter the list, the better.

Buy Organic

With all food, buy organic whenever possible. Conventional, chemical-based farming, which developed after World War II, is all about quantity—growing as much food as possible. Farmers and crops that use nitrogen fertilizer become dependent on pesticides, herbicides, and fungicides. Conventional farming routinely uses hundreds of these chemicals. Designed to kill bugs, weeds, and plant diseases, these poisons stay on our food, are eaten by birds, go into our water, are carried by the air, and are pretty much everywhere on the planet now, from the Arctic to the tropics. If you want to avoid eating these chemicals, choose organic.

Government guidelines set "safe" levels for the amount of poisonous residue that can linger on our food and be ingested on a daily basis. These levels, however, are set for individual foods and are based on what is considered "safe" for a normal, healthy adult —not for a baby or toddler, or an old person, or someone with a compromised immune system. This means there is an acceptable amount of poison that can be on the apple you give to your toddler, but the government guidelines don't take into account the fact that he is little—and they don't consider the cocktail of chemicals he eats over the course of each day by combining different foods.

Organic food, on the other hand, is about quality. It's about growing healthy soil, healthy plants, and healthy animals to create healthy people. Organic doesn't depend on chemical fertilizers or poisons to grow food or resolve problems in farming. It doesn't wage war on nature—a war, I think, we'll never win. Emerging research funded by the European Union also shows that organic food contains higher levels of some nutrients, including vitamin C; essential minerals, such as calcium, magnesium, and iron; cancer-fighting antioxidants; and omega-3 fats. If you want the best-quality food, buy organic. It's that simple. If you're unable to buy all organic, then choose organic for the things your family eats the most of and buy organic meat, eggs, and dairy products.

Genetically Modified Foods

A genetically modified (GM) food is any ingredient whose DNA has been artificially altered in a laboratory to achieve a desired characteristic. Some crops are modified to make them resistant to drought or to frost. Others have been developed to produce built-in pesticides to ward off pests and diseases, and they cannot be washed off before the food is eaten.

GM foods are often given genes from completely different food sources. This raises the question of whether a GM soybean engineered with nut proteins to boost the bean's omega-3 fats could pose a danger to someone with a nut allergy. And it's not just the harm to humans that has many worried about GM. Little can be done to prevent a field planted with GM crops from contaminating neighboring non-GM crops; and almost no testing has been done to determine the effects of genetic modification on other species in the ecosystem.

GM foods were introduced into the food chain in the 1990s, so it's still too soon to know what the lasting effects of these foods will be on our health, environment, and economies. There's no reason you and your child should eat them and be part of a massive experiment on public health. GM foods are labeled in some countries. Find out if they are in yours and then avoid them. If GM foods are not labeled where you live, then that's another reason to buy organic, which excludes GM completely.

Cooking from Scratch

Now that you understand why good, natural, organic food is so important, it's time to get started. If you're worried that cooking from scratch will be too hard or too much work, stop worrying. The recipes in this book are easy, provide your baby with the best possible nutrition, and taste a lot better than jarred baby foods.

BATCH COOKING: If you can, cook up a big batch of different dishes, freeze them in ice-cube trays and then transfer them to airtight, freezerproof containers for later use. Little cubes of food defrost quickly (see page 18), and having a variety of different foods on hand will make feeding your baby much easier.

BALANCED MEALS: Serving good, balanced meals really is easy, and the pages that follow will cover all the basics. In general, you want to make sure to serve protein, vegetables, fruit, complex carbohydrate, good oils, and filtered water every day. Protein, made of amino acids, provides the building blocks for our bodies and forms the basis of our cells. Growing children need more protein than adults. Complex carbohydrates, such as whole grains, wholewheat breads, and unpeeled white and sweet potatoes, provide steady energy. Avoid simple carbohydrates, such as white flour and white rice, and sugar, because they all wreak havoc on blood sugar levels.

Ingredients & Equipment

Whether it's food or utensils made of certain materials, I try to make sure everything I cook with is safe for my children. Here are some of my essentials:

WHOLE GRAINS: One of the most important items in my cupboards, whole grains add richness and variety to your diet. They can help lower the risk of type 2 diabetes and have been shown to protect against childhood asthma. Most people eat wheat and corn regularly, and perhaps some rye, but it's important to rotate these with other whole grains, such as brown rice, barley, quinoa, spelt, Kamut, millet, amaranth, and buckwheat. You can bake with these grains, make stews, pancakes, breads, desserts—the list is endless. I strongly suggest buying only organic whole grains. Nonorganic grains carry pesticide residues and higher levels of naturally occurring mycotoxins, which may cause illness.

Unfortunately, many people go days or longer without eating any whole grains. A grain is whole when it still contains the bran, germ, and endosperm. The bran and germ of the grain are rich in fiber, vitamins, minerals, antioxidants, and healthy fats. The endosperm is high in simple carbohydrates and low in nutrients. When grain is refined, the bran and germ are removed, leaving just the endosperm—so that's what you get in white bread and white pasta. The body quickly breaks down the endosperm's simple sugars and releases them into the bloodstream. This is one reason why eating refined grains and refined grain products, such as white flour, white bread, white rice, and white pasta, has such a harsh effect on blood sugar levels and energy. Unlike whole grains, these products have been so processed that all the natural goodness, including the fiber, has been taken out. If you look at their labels, you'll see that thiamine, niacin, and B vitamins have been added back in—but these are synthetic vitamins, not natural ones, and we don't know how good they are. Natural is always better.

It's fine to have some white pasta or a crusty baguette every now and again. But if you have white toast for breakfast, a white-bread sandwich for lunch, white-flour cookies in the afternoon and white pasta for supper, day after day and week after week, then you're getting too little nutrition—and too much wheat.

Wheat has been so hybridized over the years that it bears little resemblance to the grain first domesticated 10,000 years ago. Hybridization, especially the intensive form practiced by modern industrial agriculture, has changed the structure and gluten level in the wheat. This, along with overconsumption, might be why so many people today have wheat sensitivities. Eating a wide variety of foods is the best way to get a broad range of nutrients, so make it a point to diversify. Buy wholegrain rye bread, brown rice crackers, and spelt or corn pasta, for example, and experiment with different flours for your baking.

WHOLEGRAIN FLOUR: When I bake, I use wholegrain spelt flour. Spelt, a relative of wheat, is an ancient grain that, unlike wheat, has not been hybridized and manipulated over the years to make it easier to harvest and use. Spelt remains as nature originally created it. For breads and cookies, I use 100 percent wholegrain spelt flour; for cakes or cupcakes,

I use a 50/50 mixture of wholegrain and white spelt flours for a lighter texture. Using wholegrain flour makes treats and snacks nutritious. You can easily change your existing recipes to use wholegrain, preferably spelt, flour. For cookies or other things that don't really rise, do a straight substitution. For cakes and breads, substitute half of the white flour with wholegrain flour.

HEALTHY FATS: Good-quality fats are essential, especially for a growing child. This might sound counter-intuitive considering how much our society focuses on low-fat foods. It's important to realize, though, not all fat is bad, and people generally aren't fat from eating too much fat. Blaming obesity on fat is too simplistic. People are fat from eating badly, eating too much of the wrong foods, and not exercising enough.

Kids need a certain amount of fat in their diets. Good fats are monounsaturated and polyunsaturated fats, which include essential fatty acids. Essential fats reduce the risk of cancer, heart disease, allergies, arthritis, eczema, depression, fatigue, infections, and more. Some of the good fats I feed my kids include olive oil, flaxseed oil, hemp seed oil, oily fish oils, and almonds and pumpkin seeds. Yogurt, which isn't very high in fat, is another great choice, so buy full-fat plain yogurt for your baby. I like to cook with butter because it's a good high-heat, natural fat, but I don't use it every day and I don't use a lot. Avoid hydrogenated fats, including margarines that are made of hydrogenated or partially hydrogenated fats. If you want to use margarines, choose organic ones, which are made with nonhydrogenated oils.

COW'S MILK ALTERNATIVES: Our bodies are designed to consume our mother's milk and then move onto solid foods. So, when a baby weans, he should get his nutrition from food, not from cow's milk. No other animal continues to drink milk after it has weaned. Because we don't need milk after weaning, we begin to lose the ability to produce our own enzymes to digest it; as we get older, milk becomes more difficult to digest. Furthermore, cow's milk is pasteurized, which means all the enzymes in it that help us to digest it have been killed.

Milk is not as great a source of calcium as many people believe, either. For calcium to be well used by the body, it must be consumed with the right balance of magnesium, and milk contains very little magnesium. Foods with a perfect calcium/magnesium balance include nuts and seeds, and vegetables, such as spinach and broccoli, so make sure your child gets lots of these foods.

If you do choose to give your child cow's milk, buy organic milk: it does not contain any antibiotic or hormone residues, and research has shown that it has higher levels of vitamin E, other antioxidants and omega-3 essential fatty acids.

Although I avoid cow's milk, other milk products can be nutritious. Cultured milk products, such as yogurt, kefir, and cheese, are fermented, making them healthier and easier to digest. Yogurt and kefir both contain live bifidus and acidophilus cultures—the good bacteria that should inhabit the gut. They ensure the body produces vitamins and enzymes, and they keep harmful bacteria and toxin levels in the body under control, preventing potential diseases. Kefir has the additional benefit of healthy yeast cultures, which help restore a better balance to the gut flora. Goat- and sheep-milk products are preferable to cow-milk products because their smaller fat globules are more easily digested.

Once a baby has weaned, he can drink water. Milk substitutes, such as oat milk, rice milk, or soymilk, are good for breakfast cereals, but use soymilk and rice milk in moderation. Soy contains isoflavones, or hormone (estrogen) mimics, which can disrupt a baby's normal hormone balance. In countries where soy and its products are consumed traditionally, they're usually fermented and eaten in small quantities—not as a substitute for animal protein. Rice milk contains low levels of arsenic, so children from one to five years should not have too much of it. If a child drinks a lot of soy or rice milk, he'll drink a lot in proportion to his body weight; as a result, he'll be exposed to more of these compounds. Give your child water to drink and let him get calcium from food.

NATURAL SUGARS: Originally used only in sweet foods, sugar is now added to many savory foods as well. Concentrated, simple sugar hits the bloodstream quickly and causes a rapid increase in blood sugar levels. This gives you an energy surge that is followed by a quick drop as the body rushes to rebalance. This stress, repeated over and over, is not good. Diabetes is the extreme form of blood sugar imbalance and has become more and more common in children and young people. Eating too much sugar and too many refined grains exacerbates the problem and increases a child's risk of developing diabetes. Furthermore, sugar that is not used by the body is converted into fat.

Giving in to your child's sugar cravings is easy, but doing so can create a lifetime addiction. Your baby is so malleable, and you mold his tastes, so start him on a different route. He doesn't know about strawberry-flavored sweetened yogurt, so serve plain. Don't sweeten sour fruits, such as raspberries—let him experience their natural flavor. Some kids like tart or sour foods, and others will develop a taste for them over time. If your child says "yuck" to something once, try again another time because his taste will change and develop. I can't believe I didn't like Brussels sprouts when I was a kid—I love them now.

White and brown sugar, glucose, molasses, honey and maple syrup are all simple sugars. Fruit contains fructose, a simple sugar, but the body must first convert fructose into glucose, which means that it releases slowly. So even though fruits contain simple sugars, they are, in general, much better than sweets and other sugars.

A special word about honey: do not give honey to babies younger than one year because it carries a slight risk of botulism.

The best sweetener is brown rice syrup, which is made up mostly of complex sugars and, therefore, releases more slowly into the bloodstream. To convert the sugar in your recipes to brown rice syrup, use ¾ cup brown rice syrup for every 1 cup sugar, and reduce liquids by ¼ cup.

You'll notice there aren't a lot of desserts in this book. That's because there's really no point in serving them, especially every day. A sugar habit is a terrible thing to create in your child. Fill him up instead with good food, not sweets that contain empty calories and no nutritional value. Serve sweets occasionally, yes, as a special treat. But daily? No. And wait as long as possible to give your child sugar. You can certainly wait until his first birthday and then let the birthday cake be his first taste of sugar. (There's a great cake recipe for you on page 159.)

Help control your child's sugar cravings by reducing the regularity of sweets. I don't give dessert after every meal because it sets up an expectation for something sweet and means some kids will fight with you by not eating their food and waiting for dessert. Take the dessert away and that problem disappears.

Finally, beware of "sugar-free" foods. More often than not, this means artificial sweeteners, such as saccharine, aspartame, and sorbitol—all of which have been linked to health problems. As much as I dislike sugar and do all I can to limit it in my children's diets, it is better than artificial sweeteners, which no one should consume.

REDUCED SALT: All foods naturally contain sodium, which our bodies need. Eating too much added salt, however, is linked to all sorts of diseases, and children's kidneys struggle if made to deal with added salt. Your child's palate is pure; help shape it by making food without added salt. Wait until after one year to introduce salt and then use it only very sparingly. If you eat out a lot, eat processed foods, or are in the habit of adding salt without really thinking about it, your own palate will need time to readjust and realize, for example, that a bowl of steamed broccoli drizzled with olive oil doesn't need salt. Vegetables don't need it, and anything with cheese doesn't usually need it. To satisfy a salt craving in an older child, offer toasted seaweed like nori as a snack.

NONTOXIC STORAGE CONTAINERS: I store and serve food in little metal containers with plastic lids that don't come into contact with the food. Other good alternatives to plastic are glass or ceramic. Plastic contains harmful chemicals, including phthalates (the softer the plastic, the higher the phthalate content). Studies by Greenpeace show that some of these chemicals might interfere with the hormone systems that regulate normal growth and reproductive development in children. Kids can also ingest hazardous chemicals from plastic toys. Plastics are difficult to recycle, too. They either sit in landfills or are burned, often emitting dioxins and heavy metals. If you do use plastic, always let the food you're storing cool completely before you put it in a plastic container to reduce the risk of anything harmful leaching into the food.

STAINLESS-STEEL COOKWARE: Good stainless-steel cookware is ideal for everyday use. It can be heated to a high temperature, you can use any utensils with it, and it lasts a long time. A well-seasoned cast-iron pan is great, too.

Nonstick cookware has its conveniences, but just like plastic, it contains harmful toxins that can seep into your child's food. Perfluorooctanoic acid, or PFOA, also known as C8, is a chemical used to bond the nonstick coating to the pan. In early 2006, the United States Environmental Protection Agency (EPA) labeled PFOA a likely carcinogen and asked eight American companies to work toward its elimination by 2015. This is why I never use nonstick cookware on a regular basis—it's just not worth the risk. If you do use it occasionally—and, I admit, it's great for making pancakes—make sure you don't heat it too high, never use metal utensils, which scrape through the coating, and always open a window or turn on an extractor fan to remove potentially toxic fumes from your kitchen.

Avoid aluminum, too. Although more research needs to be done, cooking with aluminum pans has been linked to Alzheimer's disease; deodorants containing aluminum have been linked to breast cancer; and aluminum has been linked to several skeletal and neurological disorders. Until this is proven or not proven, I think it's best avoided.

OTHER EQUIPMENT: A good blender or small food processor is essential. You'll use it for everything from pureeing baby food to making things like smoothies and bread crumbs. Get yourself a good all-around vegetable knife and an inexpensive vegetable scrubber. You shouldn't peel vegetables because much of the fiber is in the skin and a lot of nutrition is just under it, so you need to scrub them.

Cooking Techniques

The recipes in this book focus heavily on nutrient-rich whole foods. Here are a few basic techniques that will help you master the art of cooking with whole foods.

SOAKING WHOLE GRAINS: In both traditional and modern cultures where whole grains are widely used, cooks take care to properly prepare them to maximize their nutrients and ease digestion. This means soaking the grain in warm, acidified water prior to cooking. It doesn't really take more time; you just have to think ahead.

All grains contain phytic acid in their outer layer. Phytic acid can combine with minerals in the intestinal tract and block absorption, leading, in time, to mineral deficiencies. Soaking grains for at least seven hours or, even better, overnight, stimulates the grain's enzymes, which break down and neutralize the phytic acid. Once neutralized, phytic acid can be an important anticancer nutrient. Soaking also partially breaks down the proteins in grains, particularly gluten, to make them easier to digest. To soak whole grains, put the amount of grain you plan to cook in a saucepan and cover with the amount of warm water stated in the recipe. Stir in one tablespoon of kefir or yogurt and leave it to soak for seven hours, or overnight, then cook without draining. If there is any history of dairy allergies in your family, rinse the grains before cooking.

DRIED BEANS: I always cook my own beans, and I never get bloated from them. The trick is to soak them overnight in double the amount of warm water and two tablespoons of lemon juice or vinegar. This rehydrates the beans and neutralizes the phytic acid and enzyme inhibitors. The next day, rinse the beans well, add fresh water for cooking, bring to a boil and boil for ten minutes, skimming any scum, which contains the difficult-to-digest complex sugars. Then add kombu, a seaweed, that helps soften the beans, makes them easier to digest, and adds nutrients and flavor.

STEAMING: If you're not going to eat vegetables raw, steaming is the best way to cook them. Steaming retains nutrients that are lost in other types of cooking. When you boil vegetables, it is very easy to overcook them and lose valuable minerals. Until babies are able to chew their food, vegetables should be steamed until completely soft; afterward, they should always be slightly crunchy.

Time to Feed Your Baby

I approach weaning and feeding my children differently from a lot of the methods out there. The truth is, no one really knows the best way to do a lot of things we have to do in life, but my method makes sense to me and has worked with my own kids.

Your baby's immune and digestive systems are still developing and are very delicate in the first two years, so start slowly. I like to start with one food at a time. This makes it easier to identify the source of any reaction your baby might have, which is harder to do if he eats four or five different foods in one day and then develops a splotchy face. If you're serving one food at time and your baby has a reaction, you can simply stop serving that particular food and try again after eight weeks to see if he can handle it.

WHEN TO INTRODUCE FOODS: Raw fruit is an excellent way to start weaning because it's gentle on the baby's system, easy to digest, and very nutritious. In addition to fruit, I recommend giving him vegetables, whole grains, legumes, and good fats from four to six months. I like to give the baby's system time to get used to solid foods, so I wait until a couple of months later to introduce fish and meats. I don't introduce grains such as wheat, rye, and spelt until one year because they contain gluten. Gluten is one of the most common proteins to which people are intolerant, so it makes sense to wait until the baby's system is more developed. Anyway, it's not like you have to give him gluten; as you will see, there is a huge range of gluten-free foods you can choose from. Eggs, cheese, nuts, and certain fruits and vegetables are introduced between 12 and 24 months. See the charts in each chapter to determine if a food is appropriate at a specific age.

If you're introducing foods in the sequence I recommend and you do sometimes have to use jarred baby food, be aware that many contain ingredients such as milk or gluten that you won't want to introduce to your baby until a certain age. Always read the labels and buy organic. Opt for plain fruit and thicken it with instant millet or brown rice flakes.

EATING ENOUGH: Babies have a strong survival instinct and will usually eat unless they're full or something is wrong, so feed your baby until he won't eat any more. Let him have a small toy at meals when he's little and he'll be happier to sit still and eat. Take the toys away when he begins feeding himself—his hands will be busy. For babies and toddlers who might not eat a lot at mealtimes, offer snacks during the day to make sure they're getting enough food and variety. You can cut out the snacking when he's older.

Not all babies are chubby; many are long and slender, so don't compare yours to others. If you're worried that he isn't eating enough, weigh him each month and plot his weight on a growth chart. As long as he stays at the same percentile, he's fine. If he's not maintaining the same percentile, consult your doctor.

STORING & REHEATING FOOD: Each recipe includes individual storage instructions, so you can plan ahead. I suggest making batches of food in the first few months and freezing them in ice-cube trays. This will save you lots of time and provide you with a variety of foods you can mix and match when you don't have the time or energy to cook fresh.

Little cubes of fruit, vegetables and grains defrost quickly, either in the fridge or heated in a pan over a medium heat, and some can be heated simply by putting the baby's bowl in a larger bowl of boiling water, which also keeps the food warm while you feed. Rice, however, should always be heated through until it is hot to kill any bacteria. Always thoroughly defrost meat, poultry, and fish cubes in the fridge before reheating.

FOOD SAFETY: I try not to get too obsessive about germs and bacteria. I think once babies are six months old, a reasonable exposure to everyday germs is a good thing because it helps to build a strong immune system. Living in a sterile environment does not. Just keep things clean, don't mix raw and cooked meats, and make sure you cook eggs and meats thoroughly for little children.

ADDING NUTRITION: We should feed ourselves the best we can all the time, but we don't, so add nutrition wherever you can. Here are some tricks to adding a little more oomph to each day. (These all must be age appropriate.)

• Always serve healthy fats (see page 13). Mix good oil into purees, pastas, or steamed veggies. Sprinkle seeds or toasted nori over rice or salads. Add chopped bean sprouts to sandwiches. Use yogurt with breakfast cereals or mix it with cucumber for a snack.

• Focus on healthy snacks, such as crispbreads, unsweetened popcorn and low-salt tortilla chips. Organic nuts, seeds and spreads, such as tahini, are great, too. Avoid peanuts, though – they're a pesticide-laden crop. If you do serve them, buy organic.

• At meals, offer two vegetables of different colors, one cooked and one raw, to provide different nutrients. You can serve one before the main dish. Vegetable sticks with olive oil, mayonnaise, mustard, or hummus for dipping are great for kids. Use ketchup occasionally but it's sweet, so don't become too dependent on it.

• Even if your child has a great diet, it's worth considering a good-quality, food-state multi-mineral and -vitamin to ensure he's getting everything he needs.

One of the biggest lessons to learn is to not get stressed. I can't say this enough to any mother—first time or third time—and I have to say it to myself all the time. Do the best you can. Have some great days, don't worry about the not-so-great ones, and strive always to improve. Establish a routine with your child when you can. His system gets used to eating, napping, and sleeping at certain times, and the steadier the routine, the easier life is! Give your child the best food you can. Try to make as many mouthfuls as you can count toward his health and well-being. He may rebel when he's older and eat junk for a while, but kids tend to go back to what they know—and what makes them feel good. Use this book to give your baby the best possible start in life, and to create health, vitality, and happiness for a lifetime.

weaning

It's hard to believe how much your baby has grown already. By four months, she might be showing signs that she's ready to start trying some solid foods. By six months, she'll definitely need to extend her culinary range beyond breast milk or formula. Her digestive system, however, is still developing, so it's important to start gently. That's why the pureed fruit, vegetables, whole grains, and legumes in this chapter are so ideal for weaning. From sweet Banana Mash and Butternut Squash Puree to nutty Baby Brown Rice Puree and creamy Flageolet Puree, these first foods will give your baby the best nutritional start. She'll love experiencing the delicious, mild flavors of these new foods—and you'll love how easy they are to prepare. This is the beginning of your child's relationship with food, so give her the best you can, with lots of variety, and she'll be on her way to a lifetime of good eating.

Avocado Mash (see page 28)

4 to 6 months

Starting your baby on her first foods is an exciting time. She can begin solids at four months, but can go for up to six months before she really needs nutrition from sources other than breast milk or formula, so don't rush to wean. The older she is, the more developed her digestive system and the better it will digest and assimilate solid foods. However, if she's grabbing your fork while you're eating, it's probably time to start, and not all babies can wait until six months. Teeth are another sign that she's ready for solids. If you offer her the first spoonful of food and it goes straight into her mouth and is swallowed, then she is definitely ready because a baby's reflex is for the tongue to push outward. This is the action for breastfeeding and also ensures she doesn't take things she shouldn't into her mouth. So if the first spoonful comes back out, she might not be ready. Even if it comes out, though, and you think that she is no longer satisfied by only breast milk or formula, you can try holding the spoon at her lips and see if she sucks the food in.

How to Wean

Your baby's immune and digestive systems are still developing and are not ready for all foods at once, so start with the ones that are most gentle and won't stress a delicate little body. The chart on page 23 lists the best foods to introduce in the first couple of months. Raw fruit is the easiest to digest, but it's important to serve vegetables early on to help your baby move away from the sweet taste of breast milk, and so you don't encourage a sweet tooth. Don't fall into the cliché of "kids don't like vegetables." Children do like vegetables, just not every vegetable all the time and not overcooked, tasteless vegetables.

REACTIONS TO FOODS: Try one food at a time for a couple of days at first. If your baby doesn't seem to like it, simply try it again after a few weeks. With each food, see if there is any reaction, such as redness in the face, repeated sneezing, or tummy upsets that cause diarrhea or constipation. If there is a reaction to a food, wait eight weeks and then try again. Her system might be able to handle it later on.

HOW MUCH TO START?: At the beginning, she might eat only one or two spoonfuls at each meal, or she might eat a whole mashed banana. It doesn't matter. It depends on your baby. Give her as much as she'll eat. If she turns her head away or won't open her mouth after one mouthful or after ten, then stop. Put the food down and distract her with a toy, then try again. Some babies eat and then need a break before taking more. If she still won't eat more, just stop and try again at the next meal. Food is new to her and her stomach is tiny. She'll gradually eat more—and you'll figure it out together. Just make sure she gets enough breast milk or formula and tries a variety of foods each week, and she will thrive and change and start to grow up before your eyes.

Introducing foods in the sequence suggested in each chapter is the best way to ensure your baby digests foods easily and thoroughly. Sometimes babies cry or get windy or doubled over from an upset tummy. Remember they have the same length of intestines we have, but theirs are crammed into a really tiny space. Eating and digesting is not always easy for them! If she is uncomfortable, gently rub your hand in a clockwise circle from her belly button downward and back up to help move the

FOODS TO BEGIN WITH AT 4 TO 6 MONTHS

Begin weaning your baby using the foods listed in the chart below. Remember to take it slowly to give your child a gentle transition to solid foods.

FRUIT*	VEGETABLES	GRAINS	LEGUMES	DAIRY & EGGS	FATS
*remove all skins	• artichoke heart	• amaranth	• flageolet bean	• kefir, only for soaking grains	• Serve 1 teaspoon per day of cold-pressed seed oil mixed with food
• apple (cooked or raw)	• beet	• brown rice	• red lentil	• yogurt, only for soaking grains	
• apricot (fresh or dried)	• broccoli	• millet			Choose from: flax hemp pumpkin safflower sesame sunflower
• avocado (after four weeks)	• butternut squash	• quinoa			
• banana	• carrot	• white rice			
• lemon juice, only for soaking legumes	• cauliflower				
• mango	• green bean				
• nectarine	• kombu, only for cooking legumes				
• papaya	• parsnip				
• peach	• pea				
• pear	• pumpkin				
• plum (fresh or dried [prune])	• rutabaga				
	• snow peas				
	• sweet potato				
	• zucchini				

food through her system. You can also try giving her cool fennel tea in a bottle or by the spoonful to help ease digestion.

IS SHE EATING ENOUGH?: If a couple of months go by and you don't think she's eating enough, plot her weight on a baby weight chart and see if she is maintaining the same percentile. If she is, don't worry. If she isn't, talk to your pediatrician. But if your baby is happy, contented, sleeps well, and doesn't cry much, then she is probably fine. If a baby is hungry, she will cry and keep on crying until you feed her.

COMFORTABLE FEEDING: If you're weaning your baby at four months, she won't be able to sit up in a chair, so feeding can be awkward. For effortless, intimate feeding at this age, sit on a soft chair or couch and, if you're right handed, put your right foot flat on the floor and cross your left leg over and rest the ankle just above your right knee. Put your baby's bottom in the hole created by your left leg and she can lean back while she eats.

RAW, STEAMED & PUREED FOOD: For this age, raw fruit should be pureed or mashed until very smooth, and dried fruit should be cooked until completely soft before pureeing. All other foods should be steamed (see page 17) until completely soft , then pureed. The pureed texture should be smooth and runny, like yogurt, without any lumps, and the food should be served warm. Think of your baby's tummy as a little cauldron with a flame underneath that needs to be kept warm. If you serve cold food, her body wastes energy heating it up before she can begin to process it. You can freeze the puree you don't immediately need in ice-cube trays, and when they're frozen, pop them out into containers that you can label and date. Then just defrost the cubes and reheat them (see page 18).

You'll find that the purees in this chapter are incredibly easy to make. You don't have to worry about weighing or measuring out most ingredients because when you're steaming, pureeing, and freezing a butternut squash, for example, it doesn't really matter how big the squash is. The more you cook at one time, though, the easier meals will be—as long as you have storage space in your freezer. I guarantee you will use everything you make. This means most of the recipes in this chapter don't make a specific number of servings. How many meals a batch of Baby Brown Rice lasts really depends on how much your baby eats and how you eventually combine it with other ingredients.

If you're not sure where to start and you do have room in your freezer, I recommend making a selection of the recipes in this chapter. Dishes such as Butternut Squash Puree, Broccoli & Cauliflower Puree, Dried Apricot Puree, Baby Brown Rice Puree, Quinoa Puree, Flageolet Puree, and Red Lentil Puree are good choices to begin with, and they provide an impressive variety you can mix and match as your baby starts to eat more.

Although the grain purees in this book are best, instant millet or brown rice flakes can be useful for thickening a meal if you accidentally water it down too much, or for mixing with baby food from a jar when traveling to make a more substantial meal.

FATS: Once your baby starts weaning, give her some good-quality oil each day. Most people are deficient in essential fatty acids, which provide vital nutrients and aid brain and nerve development. Hemp oil is the only common seed oil that meets all known essential fatty acid needs, but other seed oils are also good. Add one teaspoon of cold-pressed oil to one meal each day. If your baby doesn't like the strong flavour of flax or hemp oil, you may find she's happier to take a milder seed oil, such as pumpkin, safflower or sesame. If there is any history of seed allergies in your family, wait until your baby is at least fifteen months old to introduce seeds and seed oils, and watch for any reaction.

MEAL PLANNER FOR BABIES AT 4 TO 6 MONTHS

Use these general guidelines to help you plan your baby's weaning schedule. Remember to take it slowly—every child is different and will want to transition to solid food at a different pace.

WEEKS 1 AND 2

BREAKFAST	MID-MORNING	LUNCH	MID-AFTERNOON	DINNER	EVENING
breast/bottle	breast/bottle	breast/bottle one fruit or vegetable 1 tsp. seed oil In week 2, add Baby Brown Rice Puree (see page 30)	breast/bottle	one fruit or vegetable	breast/bottle

FROM WEEK 3

BREAKFAST	MID-MORNING	LUNCH	MID-AFTERNOON	DINNER	EVENING
breast/bottle Baby Brown Rice Puree (see page 30) or Millet Puree (see page 33) one fruit 1 tsp. seed oil	breast/bottle	breast/bottle one vegetable one bean	breast/bottle	breast/bottle Quinoa Puree (see page 33) or Amaranth Puree (see page 32) one vegetable	breast/bottle

apple puree

PREPARATION TIME:
5 minutes

STORAGE:
Refrigerate up to 3 days or freeze cubes of the puree up to 3 months.

Raw fruit is the easiest food for your baby to digest—and it is packed with nutrition. You can also use this recipe for apricot, mango, nectarine, papaya, peach, pear, or plum purees. Each fruit is great on its own as a snack or mixed with a grain puree for a healthy breakfast.

1 apple, peeled, cored, and chopped

1 Put the apple in a blender and blend 1 minute until smooth, adding a little water if the mixture is too dry.

2 Serve immediately to prevent the apple from discoloring.

apples are so common that we often overlook them. Don't! They combine antioxidants, flavanoids, and fiber in a way that's superior to other fruit. Much of the goodness is in the skin. Peel them now, but leave the skin on once your baby can chew it—around 9 months.

dried apricot puree

PREPARATION TIME:
3 minutes, plus overnight soaking

COOKING TIME:
15 minutes

STORAGE:
Refrigerate up to 3 days or freeze cubes of the cooled puree up to 3 months.

Apricots sweeten food in a nutritious way and are a good source of beta-carotene. You can use prunes for this recipe, too. It's good to have some of these dense purees on hand as ice cubes that you can quickly defrost and serve warm when hunger suddenly strikes.

1 cup unsulfured dried apricots

1 Put the apricots and 1½ cups water in a small saucepan and leave to soak, covered, overnight.

2 Bring the apricots and soaking water to a boil over high heat, then reduce the heat to low and simmer, covered, 15 minutes, stirring occasionally, or until completely soft. If using a blender with a plastic container, leave the mixture to cool completely before blending.

3 Transfer the mixture to a blender and blend 1 minute until smooth. Serve warm, reheating if necessary.

▲ banana mash

MAKES:
1 serving

PREPARATION
TIME:
3 minutes

STORAGE:
Use immediately.
Not suitable for
storage.

My daughter Cassie couldn't get enough of this mash. Banana makes a great emergency food, especially if your baby wakes up hungry at night.

1 banana, peeled

1 Put the banana on a plate and mash, using a fork, until it forms a smooth paste, adding a little water if necessary. For a smoother consistency, chop the banana into pieces, put it in a blender and blend, adding a little water if necessary, 1 minute until smooth.

2 Serve immediately to prevent the banana from discoloring.

bananas
are one of nature's best sources of potassium, which helps to regulate salt in the body. The potassium in bananas is also particularly valuable when your baby has diarrhea. Their pectin content, on the other hand, can help to relieve constipation.

avocado mash

MAKES:
1 serving

PREPARATION TIME:
3 minutes

STORAGE:
Use immediately. Not suitable for storage.

Probably the healthiest fruit, avocado is satisfying, nourishing, and easy to digest. It also contains the best fat you can give your little one. It's been one of my daughter Jessie's favourites since she was tiny.

½ avocado, pitted

1 Scoop the avocado flesh into a blender and add enough warm water to cover halfway.

2 Blend 1 minute until smooth, adding more water if necessary. Serve immediately to prevent the avocado from discoloring.

avocados are so packed with nutrition they can be thought of as a complete food. They are full of fiber, potassium, and B vitamins, as well as important monounsaturated fatty acids, which might help boost memory.

artichoke heart puree

PREPARATION TIME:
10 minutes

COOKING TIME:
45 minutes

STORAGE:
Refrigerate up to 3 days or freeze cubes of the cooled puree up to 3 months.

This lovely puree is a nice way to introduce your baby to artichokes. Add them in small quantities to other dishes until your baby is a toddler, and old enough to enjoy them roasted or baked.

2 globe artichokes, stems removed

1 Put the artichokes in a steamer and steam, covered, over boiling water 45 minutes, or until a leaf pulled from the top comes out easily. Add extra boiling water during steaming, if necessary. Remove from the heat and set aside until cool enough to handle, reserving the steam water.

2 Peel the leaves off the artichokes and reserve them to serve as an appetizer for yourself dipped in olive oil or melted butter. Using a sharp knife, carefully cut out and discard the hairy chokes, then chop the artichoke hearts and transfer them to a blender (leaving them to cool completely first if using a blender with a plastic container). Add enough of the reserved steam water to cover the artichoke hearts halfway. Blend 1 minute until smooth. Serve warm, reheating if necessary.

carrot puree

PREPARATION TIME:
10 minutes

COOKING TIME:
25 minutes

STORAGE:
Refrigerate up to 3 days or freeze cubes of the cooled puree up to 3 months.

You can use vegetables like peas, zucchini, and unpeeled parsnips and sweet potatoes in this recipe, although you'll need to watch cooking times and reduce the time for zucchini (15 minutes) and peas (7 minutes).

6 carrots, unpeeled, but topped and tailed

1 Cut the carrots in half lengthwise and then into 1-inch pieces. Put them in a steamer and steam, covered, over boiling water 20 to 25 minutes until completely soft. Reserve the steam water. If using a blender with a plastic container, leave the carrots to cool completely before blending.

2 Transfer the carrots to a blender and add enough of the steam water to cover them halfway. Blend 1 minute until smooth. Serve warm, reheating if necessary.

broccoli & cauliflower puree

PREPARATION TIME:
10 minutes

COOKING TIME:
10 minutes

STORAGE:
Refrigerate up to 3 days or freeze cubes of the cooled puree up to 3 months.

You can cook these separately, but mixing them together makes a great combination. Save the broccoli stem for yourself: simply cut off the hard skin and enjoy the sweet center raw or lightly steamed.

½ cup broccoli cut into 1¼in. florets
½ cup cauliflower cut into 1¼in. florets

1 Put the broccoli and cauliflower in a steamer and steam, covered, over boiling water 10 minutes, or until completely soft. Reserve the steam water. If using a blender with a plastic container, leave the vegetables to cool completely before blending.

2 Transfer the vegetables to a blender and add enough of the steam water to cover them halfway. Blend 1 minute until smooth. Serve warm, reheating if necessary.

butternut squash puree ▶

PREPARATION TIME:
10 minutes

COOKING TIME:
30 minutes

STORAGE:
Refrigerate up to 3 days or freeze cubes of the cooled puree up to 3 months.

Squash and pumpkin are my favorite first vegetables. They have a lovely sweetness and are easily digested by delicate, tiny stomachs. Use this recipe for beets, green beans, snow peas, and peeled rutabaga and turnip, too.

1 butternut squash, peeled, seeded, and cut into 2in. cubes

1 Put the squash in a steamer and steam, covered, over boiling water 30 minutes, or until completely soft. Reserve the steam water. If using a blender with a plastic container, leave the squash to cool completely before blending.

2 Transfer the squash to a blender and add enough of the steam water to cover it halfway. Blend 1 minute until smooth. Serve warm, reheating if necessary.

butternut squash

is sweet, filling, and incredibly versatile. Its lovely hue comes from its beta-carotene content, which rivals even that of mangoes and cantaloupe.

baby brown rice puree

PREPARATION TIME:
5 minutes, plus at least 7 hours soaking

COOKING TIME:
1 hour

STORAGE:
Refrigerate up to 1 day or freeze cubes of the cooled puree up to 1 month. Reheat until hot.

Many parents buy white rice or brown rice flakes, but your baby gets much better nutrition when you make your own brown rice puree.

½ cup brown basmati rice
1 tsp. kefir or plain yogurt

1 Put the rice, kefir, and 2½ cups plus 2 tablespoons warm water in a medium saucepan and leave to soak, covered, 7 hours, or overnight.

2 Bring to a boil over high heat, then reduce the heat to low and simmer, covered, 1 hour, or until the rice is very tender. If using a blender with a plastic container, leave the rice to cool completely before blending.

3 Transfer the rice to a blender and blend 1 minute until smooth. Serve warm, reheating if necessary.

kefir

is a fermented milk product that contains beneficial bacteria and yeast cultures, which aid digestion and promote the development of good probiotic flora in the gut.

▲ amaranth puree

Variety is so important in a baby's diet. Adding amaranth into your rotation of grains gives you choice and a new mix of minerals and vitamins. It has a lovely flavor and can be combined with anything.

PREPARATION TIME:
5 minutes, plus at least 7 hours soaking

COOKING TIME:
40 minutes

STORAGE:
Refrigerate up to 3 days or freeze cubes of the cooled puree up to 3 months.

½ cup amaranth
1 tsp. kefir or plain yogurt

1 Put the amaranth, kefir, and 2 cups warm water in a medium saucepan and leave to soak, covered, 7 hours, or overnight.

2 Bring to a boil over high heat, then reduce the heat to low and cook, covered, 40 minutes, stirring occasionally so it doesn't clump to the bottom of the pan. If using a blender with a plastic container, leave the amaranth to cool completely before blending.

3 Transfer the amaranth to a blender and blend 1 minute until smooth. Serve warm, reheating if necessary.

millet puree

Millet is a slightly bitter grain. Try it first with nonsweet vegetables and if your baby doesn't like it, try it with either sweet vegetables or fruit.

PREPARATION TIME:
5 minutes, plus at least 7 hours soaking

COOKING TIME:
45 minutes

STORAGE:
Refrigerate up to 3 days or freeze cubes of the cooled puree up to 3 months.

½ cup millet
1 tsp. kefir or plain yogurt

1 Put the millet, kefir, and 3 cups warm water in a medium saucepan and leave to soak, covered, 7 hours, or overnight.

2 Bring to a boil over high heat. Skim any scum that rises to the surface, then reduce the heat to low and simmer, covered, 45 minutes, or until completely soft. If using a blender with a plastic container, leave the millet to cool completely before blending.

3 Transfer the millet to a blender and blend 1 minute until smooth. Serve warm, reheating if necessary.

millet is one of the oldest foods known and possibly the first cereal grain used. It is alkaline and helps balance acidity in the body. It is also easy to digest, helps bowel function, and is calming.

quinoa puree

Quinoa, the highest protein grain, is an excellent grain to add to your repertoire and adds variety to your baby's diet. Quinoa must be soaked, as in this recipe, or toasted as in the recipe on page 47 before cooking.

PREPARATION TIME:
5 minutes, plus at least 7 hours soaking

COOKING TIME:
40 minutes

STORAGE:
Refrigerate up to 3 days or freeze cubes of the cooled puree up to 3 months.

½ cup quinoa
1 tsp. kefir or plain yogurt

1 Put the quinoa, kefir, and 1¾ cups warm water in a medium saucepan and leave to soak, covered, 7 hours, or overnight.

2 Bring to a boil over high heat, then reduce the heat to low and simmer, covered, 40 minutes, or until the quinoa is very tender. If using a blender with a plastic container, leave the quinoa to cool completely before blending.

3 Transfer the quinoa to a blender and blend 1 minute until smooth. Serve warm, reheating if necessary.

white rice puree

PREPARATION TIME:
5 minutes

COOKING TIME:
30 minutes

STORAGE:
Refrigerate up to 1 day or freeze cubes of the cooled puree up to 1 month. Reheat until hot.

I always prefer whole grains, but white rice is the least allergenic food and is very gentle on the digestive tract. It's ideal if your little one has had an upset tummy—or has a medical reason not to eat whole grains.

½ cup white basmati rice

1 Put the rice and 1¾ cups water in a medium saucepan, cover, and bring to a boil over high heat. Reduce the heat to low and cook 30 minutes, or until very soft. If using a blender with a plastic container, leave the rice to cool completely before blending.

2 Transfer the rice to a blender and blend 1 minute until smooth. Serve warm, reheating if necessary.

red lentil puree

PREPARATION TIME:
5 minutes, plus overnight soaking

COOKING TIME:
55 minutes

STORAGE:
Refrigerate up to 3 days or freeze cubes of the cooled puree up to 3 months.

Lentils are easy to digest and add protein to a meal. They're a great staple to have in your freezer to bulk up baby meals. Use up to three frozen cubes mixed with rice and vegetables.

½ cup split red lentils
2 tsp. lemon juice

1 Put the lentils and lemon juice in a medium saucepan, cover with water, and leave to soak, covered, overnight.

2 Drain and rinse the lentils. Return them to the pan, add 2 cups water and bring to a boil over high heat 10 minutes, skimming any scum that rises to the surface. Reduce the heat to low and cook, covered, 45 minutes, or until completely soft. If using a blender with a plastic container, leave the mixture to cool completely before blending.

3 Transfer the lentils and cooking liquid to a blender and blend 1 minute until smooth. Serve warm, reheating if necessary.

red lentils are nutritional giants packed with protein, high amounts of six minerals, and two B vitamins. Their high fiber content prevents blood sugar levels from rising quickly.

▼ flageolet puree

PREPARATION TIME:
5 minutes, plus overnight soaking

COOKING TIME:
2 hours 10 minutes

STORAGE:
Refrigerate up to 3 days or freeze cubes of the cooled puree up to 3 months.

Cooking legumes with kombu, a vitamin- and mineral-packed seaweed, helps make them more easily digestible, especially for tiny tummies.

scant ½ cup dried flageolet beans
2 tsp. lemon juice
1 strip of kombu, about 3¼ x 2in.

1 Put the beans and lemon juice in a medium saucepan, cover with water, and leave to soak, covered, overnight.

2 Drain and rinse the beans. Return the beans to the pan and add 2½ cups water. Bring to a boil over high heat and boil 10 minutes, skimming any scum that rises to the surface. Reduce the heat to low, add the kombu, and cook, covered, 2 hours, or until completely soft, then discard the kombu. If using a blender with a plastic container, leave the mixture to cool completely before blending.

3 Transfer the beans and cooking liquid to a blender and blend 1 minute until smooth, adding a little more water if necessary. Serve warm, reheating if necessary.

three meals a day

If you've waited for your baby to reach six months before weaning, follow chapter 1 before advancing to the recipes in this chapter. If he's already getting used to eating from a spoon, it's time to make things even more interesting by combining flavors. His digestive system is ready for lots of new foods, too. Although he's still consuming breast milk or formula, a good percentage of his calories is now coming from other foods—so high-quality protein is important. A bigger variety of legumes and the introduction of fish, poultry, and meat make it easy to create exciting meals. Quinoa & Coconut Oatmeal, succulent Sardines & Sweet Potato and savoury-sweet Navy Beans with Beets are just a few new options. Try mixing and matching different foods, too—you might stumble upon a combination he'll absolutely love.

Navy Beans & Beets (see page 46)

6 to 9 months

If your baby hasn't started weaning yet, six months is the time to start. Begin with chapter 1 first and then start introducing the foods in this chapter.

Your baby's first teeth may have already appeared, and if they haven't, they will soon. Either way, he's probably showing a much greater interest in chewing. At this stage, his food should still be pureed, but you can gradually start to leave it a little lumpier by pureeing for a shorter time or simply mashing it with a fork. If you give your baby lumpier food and he starts pooping out lumps, go back to smoother purees until he's chewing more. Don't worry if he isn't chewing yet. It will just happen later, when he's ready.

GRATED FOOD & FOOD PIECES: Once he is chewing lumps, you can start introducing some exciting new textures by mixing finely grated, raw fiber and vegetables into his food. This will encourage him to chew more—without the risk of choking. Because you're grating fruit so finely, you can also start to include the skins, which have great nutritional value. Along with the lumpier purees, you can now offer your baby little pieces, about ¼ inch in size, of well-cooked vegetables or soft raw fruit (without skins), too. Not only does this encourage him to chew, it also encourages him to feed himself. He can start munching on tiny bits at the table while you are cooking or heating up the main course.

If your baby is just starting to chew, let him try some puffed rice. It's small, dissolves in the mouth easily, and is good for hand-eye coordination. If your baby is teething and chewing well, and you want to give him something to really chew on, start with unsalted brown rice cakes. They're healthy and they disintegrate easily. Avoid commercially available baby crackers, which are made of white flour and sugar and have little nutritional value.

CONTINUING WITH BREAST MILK OR FORMULA: Your baby will now be having three good meals each day, but you should carry on giving him breast milk or formula at breakfast and between meals because it's still an important source of protein for him. Give him as much solid food as he'll eat at breakfast first and then finish the meal off with some breast milk or formula. Between meals, when he isn't having solid foods, let him take as much breast milk as he wants; if you're giving him formula instead, follow the instructions on the package to determine how much is appropriate for this age.

DRINKS: Now that he's having his milk between meals and the purees are becoming more substantial and less watery, you can start to offer a little water at mealtimes. Unless you have well water and don't live an area where intensive agriculture is leaching chemicals into your well, I suggest filtering tap water to remove the worst of the chemicals and unwanted metals that might be in there. Make sure to serve his water slightly warm so it doesn't chill the stomach. Drinking water is a great habit to get your child into, and it's one of the healthiest drinks you can give him.

I don't offer diluted fruit juices because I think the nutritional benefit is minimal—he's much better off eating pureed or mashed fruit instead. Most babies are attracted to anything sweet, but this can lead to a sugar addiction (see page 14), which is hard for anyone to break. You also don't want his stomach to fill up with sweet juice instead of food. When he's older, you might want to give him juice as an occasional treat, but at this age it's best to focus on making sure his calories come from eating nutritious whole foods.

NEW FOODS TO INTRODUCE AT 6 TO 9 MONTHS

Your child is now ready for the foods listed in the chart below. Combine them with the foods listed in the previous chapter to give him the best variety you can.

GRAINS	LEGUMES	NUTS & SEEDS	FISH	POULTRY & MEATS*	FATS
• buckwheat	• black bean • black-eyed peas • fava bean (no skins) • cannellini bean • chickpea • lentil, including brown, green, and Puy • mung bean • navy or great northern bean • pinto bean	• coconut	• anchovy (fresh not canned) • mackerel • salmon • sardine	* Serve all poultry and meats in small amounts only • beef and other red meats • poultry • venison and other game	• olive oil

PROTEIN: Your baby is growing and developing quickly, so protein is becoming more important now, especially as he begins reducing the amount of milk he drinks. His digestive system is getting used to more foods and is ready for slightly heavier ones, such as fish and meats, which are great sources of protein. I try to give different proteins three times a day, but if I manage it only twice, that's okay.

FISH: You can now introduce fish, which can be an excellent source of essential fatty acids. Be aware, however, that many kinds of fish carry toxins, including dioxins and polychlorinated biphenyls (PCBs), from the poisons we dump into our waterways. So the lower down the food chain you eat the better. By this I mean, eat small fish instead of big fish. Small fish that eat plankton accumulate far fewer toxins in their flesh than large carnivorous fish, such as tuna, that eat lots and lots of little fish and, as a result, build up more toxins. The best fish to eat are fresh anchovies (not canned ones because they're too salty) and any sardines. These are also good because their tiny, soft bones provide calcium, but do not pose a choking risk. Avoid conventionally farmed fish, which is raised in poor, crowded conditions. Some varieties of organic fish are available. Although they must be farmed to maintain organic standards, they are raised in the best environment and given the best feed possible, so this is the only farmed fish worth eating. Look for sustainably sourced seafood, too, which is caught using methods that have a less severe impact on the ecosystem. Suppliers of sustainably fished seafood do not deplete already-threatened populations of fish, trap unwanted fish and dolphins in vast nets, or trawl the ocean floor, causing irreparable damage. They are good alternatives to overfished varieties. Try pollock and haddock, for example, instead of overfished cod.

POULTRY & MEAT: You can also introduce poultry and meat. Organic poultry and red meats are, without question, the best, because they do not contain growth hormones or antibiotic residues. Game is next best because it is wild, lean, and not subjected to the unpleasantries of conventional farming practices. If organic meat doesn't suit your budget, buy a little when you can and then provide protein through grain and bean combinations. Remember, variety is always the best policy anyway, and eating less meat is better not only for human health but for the health of our environment. Make sure all poultry and meats are thoroughly cooked through to avoid any problems with bacteria.

COCONUT: Coconut has good fats and provides a new texture and delicious flavour. Wait, however, until 15–24 months to introduce other nuts and seeds. As always, watch for any reaction in your child. If there is one, wait eight weeks and then try again.

FATS: Continue adding two teaspoons cold-pressed oil to your baby's food each day—or feed it to him by the teaspoonful if he'll take it. His brain and nervous system are still developing, and the essential fats in these oils are extremely important.

MEAL PLANNER FOR BABIES AT 6–9 MONTHS

This planner ensures that your baby eats a mixture of grains, fiber and vegetables each day and through the week. Breast milk or formula still provides good protein.

DAY	BREAKFAST	MID-MORNING	LUNCH	MID-AFTERNOON	TEA	EVENING
1	Millet Puree (see page 33) Apple Puree (see page 26) with 2 tsp. seed oil breast/bottle	breast/bottle	Baby Brown Rice Puree (see page 30) Avocado Mash (see page 28) warm water	breast/bottle	Sardines & Sweet Potato (see page 49) warm water	breast/bottle
2	Amaranth Puree (see page 32) Dried Apricot Puree (see page 26) with 2 tsp. seed oil breast/bottle	breast/bottle	Buckwheat & Carrot (see page 43) with 2 tsp. olive oil warm water	breast/bottle	Beef & Cauliflower (see page 50) warm water	breast/bottle
3	Quinoa & Coconut Oatmeal (page 42) pear puree (see Apple Puree on page 26) with 2 tsp. seed oil breast/bottle	breast/bottle	Puy Lentils & Butternut Squash (see page 43) with 2 tsp. olive oil warm water	breast/bottle	Mackerel & Broccoli (see page 49) warm water	breast/bottle
4	Rice & Mango Breakfast (see page 42) with 2 tsp. seed oil breast/bottle	breast/bottle	Navy Beans & Beets (see page 46) with 2 tsp. olive oil warm water	breast/bottle	Chicken & Zucchini (see page 51) warm water	breast/bottle
5	Millet Puree (see page 33) Banana Mash (see page 27) with 2 tsp. seed oil breast/bottle	breast/bottle	Mung Beans with Toasted Quinoa (see page 47) with 2 tsp. olive oil warm water	breast/bottle	Venison & Parsnip (see page 50) warm water	breast/bottle
6	Quinoa Puree (see page 33) papaya puree (see Apple Puree on page 26) breast/bottle	breast/bottle	Fava Bean & Pumpkin Puree (see page 45) with 2 tsp. seed oil warm water	breast/bottle	Black-Eyed Peas & Brown Rice (see page 45) with 2 tsp. olive oil warm water	breast/bottle
7	Baby Brown Rice Puree (see page 30) plum puree (see Apple Puree on page 26) with 2 tsp. seed oil breast/bottle	breast/bottle	Pinto Beans, Millet & Avocado (see page 44) warm water	breast/bottle	Salmon & Peas (see page 48) warm water	breast/bottle

quinoa & coconut oatmeal

"Oatmeal" can be made not only with oats. Try amaranth, brown rice, buckwheat, millet, and quinoa when you need creative breakfast ideas.

MAKES:
2 servings

PREPARATION TIME:
5 minutes, plus overnight soaking and making the apricot puree

COOKING TIME:
40 minutes

STORAGE:
Refrigerate up to 3 days or freeze cubes of the cooled puree up to 3 months.

½ cup quinoa
2 tbsp. flaked coconut
1 tbsp. kefir or plain yogurt
2 tsp. Dried Apricot Puree (see page 26), to serve

1 Put the quinoa, coconut, kefir, and 1½ cups warm water in a medium saucepan and leave to soak, covered, overnight.

2 Bring the mixture to a boil over high heat, then reduce the heat to low and simmer, covered, 40 minutes, or until the quinoa is very soft. If using a blender with a plastic container, leave the mixture to cool completely before blending.

3 Transfer the mixture to a blender and blend 1 minute until smooth. Serve warm with the dried apricot puree, reheating if necessary.

rice & mango breakfast

This is one of Nicholas's favorite breakfasts. The brown rice flakes are a wonderful alternative to rolled oats. They cook more quickly than brown rice, making this delicious dish perfect for mornings when you're pushed for time.

MAKES:
4 servings

PREPARATION TIME:
10 minutes, plus overnight soaking

COOKING TIME:
10 minutes

STORAGE:
Refrigerate the mango puree up to 3 days or freeze in cubes up to 3 months. Refrigerate the cooled cereal for up to 1 day. Reheat until hot.

½ cup brown rice flakes
1 tbsp. kefir or plain yogurt
1 mango, peeled, seeded, and chopped
¼ apple, peeled and grated, to serve

1 Put the rice flakes, kefir, and ¾ cup warm water in a medium saucepan and leave to soak, covered, overnight.

2 Bring the mixture to a simmer over medium heat, then reduce the heat to low and cook 10 minutes, stirring occasionally, or until the rice flakes are very soft.

3 Meanwhile, put the mango in a blender and blend 1 minute, or until smooth. Stir the pureed mango into the rice flakes, then sprinkle with the grated apple. Serve warm.

mango is high in iron, vitamin E, beta-carotene, and selenium. It's a deliciously sweet fruit that's great for aiding digestion and balancing acidity in the body.

buckwheat & carrot

Buckwheat's strong flavor is balanced here by sweet carrot. Some babies will love this on its own as a main course; others will prefer it as a side dish.

MAKES:
4 servings

PREPARATION TIME:
5 minutes, plus at least 7 hours soaking

COOKING TIME:
25 minutes

STORAGE:
Refrigerate up to 3 days or freeze cubes of the cooled puree up to 3 months.

2 tbsp. buckwheat
1 tsp. kefir or plain yogurt
1 carrot, quartered lengthwise and cut into ¼in. pieces

1 Put the buckwheat, kefir, and ¾ cup warm water in a small saucepan and leave to soak, covered, at room temperature at least 7 hours, or overnight.

2 Add the carrot, cover, and bring to a boil over high heat. Reduce the heat to low and simmer, covered, 25 minutes. Leave to cool slightly, then serve warm. If desired, transfer the mixture to a blender (leaving the mixture to cool completely before blending if using a blender with a plastic container), then blend 1 minute until smooth before serving warm, reheating if necessary.

puy lentils & butternut squash

This beautiful combination of savory lentils and naturally sweet butternut squash is sure to become a favorite with your baby.

MAKES:
4 servings

PREPARATION TIME:
10 minutes, plus overnight soaking

COOKING TIME:
1 hour 5 minutes

STORAGE:
Refrigerate up to 3 days or freeze cubes of the cooled puree up to 3 months.

½ cup Puy lentils
2 tsp. lemon juice
1 small butternut squash, peeled, seeded, and cut into 1in. cubes
1 tbsp. olive oil

1 Put the lentils and lemon juice in a medium saucepan, cover with warm water, and leave to soak, covered, overnight.

2 Drain and rinse the lentils. Return them to the pan and add 1½ cups water. Bring to a boil over high heat and boil 10 minutes, skimming any scum that rises to the surface. Reduce the heat to low and cook, covered, 1 hour, or until completely soft.

3 Meanwhile, preheat the oven to 400°F. Put the squash in a shallow baking dish, drizzle with the olive oil, and toss to coat. Bake 30 to 40 minutes until very soft and light brown. Remove from the oven. If using a blender with a plastic container, leave the squash and lentils to cool completely before blending.

4 Transfer the squash, lentils, and cooking liquid to a blender. Blend 1 minute until smooth. Serve warm, reheating if necessary.

▲ pinto beans, millet & avocado

I love avocado with anything. Serving it with creamy pinto beans makes it a more substantial meal for your growing baby.

MAKES:
4 servings

PREPARATION TIME:
5 minutes, plus overnight soaking and making the avocado and millet

COOKING TIME:
2 hours 10 minutes

STORAGE:
Refrigerate up to 3 days or freeze cubes of the cooled bean puree up to 3 months.

¼ cup dried pinto beans
2 tsp. lemon juice
1 strip of kombu, about 3¼ x 2in.
1 recipe quantity Avocado Mash (see page 28)
4 portions Millet Puree (see page 33)

1 Put the beans and lemon juice in a medium saucepan, cover with warm water, and leave to soak, covered, overnight.

2 Drain and rinse the beans. Return them to the pan and add 1¼ cups water. Bring to a boil over high heat and boil 10 minutes, skimming any scum that rises to the surface. Reduce the heat to low, add the kombu and cook, covered, 2 hours, or until the beans are completely soft, then discard the kombu. If using a blender with a plastic container, leave the mixture to cool completely before blending.

3 Transfer the mixture to a blender and blend 1 minute until smooth. Serve warm with the avocado mash and millet puree, or mix all three purees together, reheating the millet and beans first if necessary.

fava bean & pumpkin puree

Sweet pumpkin goes well with anything, and combined with fresh fava beans, it's simply amazing. Fava beans are a particularly special treat when they're in season because they're so fresh tasting.

MAKES:
4 servings

PREPARATION TIME:
10 minutes, plus making the pumpkin puree

COOKING TIME:
10 minutes

STORAGE:
Refrigerate up to 3 days or freeze cubes of the cooled bean puree up to 3 months.

16 fava bean pods
2 portions pumpkin puree (see Butternut Squash Puree, page 30)

1 Slit each bean pod along its seam and pop the beans out. Bring a small saucepan of water to a boil over high heat, add the beans, and boil 10 minutes, or until soft. Remove from the heat, drain, and leave to cool, then peel the beans and discard the tough skins.

2 Transfer the beans to a blender and add enough water to cover halfway. Blend 1 minute until smooth.

3 Put the pumpkin puree and 1 to 2 tablespoons water in a pan and heat over medium heat until warm, then stir in the fava bean puree. Serve warm.

black-eyed peas & brown rice

A classic vegetarian protein, the combination of beans and rice forms a complete protein that has all the essential amino acids the body needs.

MAKES:
4 servings

PREPARATION TIME:
5 minutes, plus overnight soaking and making the brown rice puree

COOKING TIME:
2 hours 10 minutes

STORAGE:
Refrigerate up to 1 day or freeze cubes of the cooled bean puree up to 3 months.

½ cup dried black-eyed peas
2 tsp. lemon juice
1 strip of kombu, about 3¼ x 2in.
4 portions Baby Brown Rice Puree (see page 30)

1 Put the beans and lemon juice in a medium saucepan, cover with warm water, and leave to soak, covered, overnight.

2 Drain and rinse the beans. Return them to the pan and add 2½ cups water. Bring to a boil over high heat and boil 10 minutes, skimming any scum that rises to the surface. Reduce the heat to low, add the kombu, and cook, covered, 2 hours, or until the beans are completely soft, then discard the kombu. If using a blender with a plastic container, leave the mixture to cool before blending.

3 Transfer the mixture to a blender and blend 1 minute until smooth. Serve warm with the rice, reheating if necessary.

navy beans & beets

Beet's natural sweetness beautifully complements haricot beans. This is a good dish to have as a side dish or to mix with a grain, such as quinoa or millet, to make a main dish.

MAKES:
4 servings

PREPARATION TIME:
10 minutes, plus overnight soaking

COOKING TIME:
1 hour 40 minutes

STORAGE:
Refrigerate up to 3 days or freeze cubes of the cooled purees up to 3 months.

½ cup dried navy or great northern beans
2 tsp. lemon juice
1 strip of kombu, about 3¼ x 2in.
4 small beets with stems trimmed to 1in., washed well without breaking the skin

1 Put the beans and lemon juice in a medium saucepan, cover with warm water, and leave to soak, covered, overnight.

2 Drain and rinse the beans. Return them to the pan and add 2½ cups water. Bring to a boil over high heat and boil 10 minutes, skimming any scum that rises to the top. Reduce the heat to low, add the kombu, and cook, covered, 1½ hours, or until the beans are completely soft, then discard the kombu. If using a blender with a plastic container, leave the mixture to cool completely before blending.

3 Meanwhile, bring a medium pan of water to the boil over high heat and add the beets, ensuring they are completely covered in water. Reduce the heat to low and simmer, covered, 45 minutes, or until the beets are completely soft and the skins come off easily. Drain and leave to stand until cool enough to handle.

4 Remove and discard the skins, then chop the beets, put them in a blender, and blend 1 minute until smooth, adding a little water, if necessary. Transfer the puree to a bowl and wash the blender.

5 Transfer the beans and cooking liquid to the blender and blend 1 minute until smooth.

6 Mix together equal quantities of the bean and beet purees. Serve warm, reheating if necessary.

beets

contains silica, which helps the body use calcium. This is important for your growing child's musculo-skeletal development and health. Beets also contains high amounts of carotenoids and flavanoids, which are important anti-oxidants.

mung beans with toasted quinoa

Mung beans are easily digested, so they're perfect for your baby. Combining beans and grains is a wonderful way to get protein, so mix and match different combinations to create a range of healthy meals.

MAKES:
4 servings

PREPARATION TIME:
5 minutes, plus overnight soaking

COOKING TIME:
1 hour 10 minutes

STORAGE:
Refrigerate up to 3 days or freeze cubes of the cooled purees up to 3 months.

½ cup dried **mung beans**
2 tsp. lemon juice
1 strip of kombu, about 3¼ x 2in.
½ cup quinoa

1 Put the beans and lemon juice in a medium saucepan, cover with warm water, and leave to soak, covered, overnight.

2 Drain and rinse the beans. Return them to the pan and add 2½ cups water. Bring to a boil over high heat and boil 10 minutes, skimming any scum that rises to the surface. Reduce the heat to low, add the kombu and cook, covered, 1 hour, or until the beans are completely soft, then discard the kombu.

3 While the beans are cooking, put the quinoa in a strainer and rinse under cold running water, then drain well. Transfer to a medium pan and toast over high heat 5 minutes, stirring continuously, until any excess water evaporates and the quinoa is slightly brown and begins to pop. Slowly add 1 cup water, cover, and bring to a boil over high heat. Reduce the heat to low and simmer 30 minutes, or until tender. If using a blender with a plastic container, leave both the quinoa and the bean mixture to cool completely before blending.

4 Transfer the bean mixture to the blender and blend 1 minute until smooth. Transfer the puree to a bowl and wash the blender.

5 Put the quinoa in the blender and blend for 1 minute until smooth.

6 Mix together equal quantities of the bean and quinoa purees. Serve warm, reheating if necessary.

mung beans are also known as green or golden gram. They are sweet, soft, and easily digestible. Low in fat, they are rich in carbohydrates and vitamins B1 and B2. Like all beans, they provide satiating bulk as your baby's appetite for solid food grows.

▲ salmon & peas

If you can get them, wild salmon and organic salmon are much better than conventionally farmed fish. The peas give this dish an intense sweetness.

MAKES:
4 servings

PREPARATION TIME:
5 minutes

COOKING TIME:
15 minutes

STORAGE:
Refrigerate up to 2 days or freeze cubes of the cooled puree up to 1 month.

2 tsp. olive oil
4oz. salmon fillet, rinsed
4 tbsp. shelled peas

1 Heat a small skillet over medium heat. Add the olive oil and when it is hot, add the salmon, skin-side up. Cook, covered, 5 minutes, then turn the fish over. Cook, covered, 5 to 10 minutes longer until cooked through. Meanwhile, put the peas in a steamer and steam, covered, over boiling water 10 minutes, or until soft.

2 When the fish has finished cooking, remove it from the heat. Remove and discard the skin and roughly chop the salmon, checking with your fingers for bones. If using a blender with a plastic container, leave both the peas and salmon to cool completely before blending.

3 Transfer the peas and salmon to a blender and add enough of the steam water to cover halfway. Blend for 1 minute until the mixture forms a lumpy puree. Serve warm, reheating if necessary.

sardines & sweet potato

Sardines really are the best type of fish, so get your baby loving them from a young age. Mixing them with sweet potato will make it easy. Cassie was a big fan of this dish from the very beginning.

MAKES:
4 servings

PREPARATION TIME:
10 minutes

COOKING TIME:
20 minutes

STORAGE:
Refrigerate up to 2 days or freeze cubes of the cooled puree up to 1 month.

1 sweet potato, unpeeled, chopped into 1in. cubes
4 canned sardines in oil or water, drained

1 Put the sweet potato in a steamer and steam, covered, over boiling water 20 minutes, or until completely soft. Remove from the heat, transfer to a bowl, and mash, using a fork.

2 In another bowl, mash the sardines and their bones well with a fork, then stir them into the sweet potato. Serve warm.

sardines
are high in omega-3 fatty acids and protein. They're also a good source of vitamin D and calcium, which work together to promote stronger bones. They're a wonderful fast food, too.

mackerel & broccoli

Your baby will love the rich texture of nutrient-rich mackerel. Serve this as suggested or mix it with a grain to add some complex carbohydrates.

MAKES:
4 servings

PREPARATION TIME:
5 minutes

COOKING TIME:
10 minutes

STORAGE:
Refrigerate up to 2 days or freeze cubes of the cooled puree up to 1 month.

½ cup broccoli cut into 1in. florets
3oz. smoked mackerel, deboned

1 Put the broccoli in a steamer and steam, covered, over boiling water 10 minutes, or until completely soft. Reserve the steam water. If using a blender with a plastic container, leave to cool completely before blending.

2 Meanwhile, remove and discard the skin from the mackerel and remove any bones, feeling the flesh with your fingers. Shred the mackerel into a small bowl with a fork.

3 Transfer the broccoli to a blender and add enough of the steam water to cover halfway. Add the mackerel and blend for 1 minute until smooth, adding more steam water if necessary. Serve warm, reheating if necessary.

mackerel
is packed with omega-3 fatty acids, selenium, and vitamins B6 and B12. Eating oily fish helps in the development of nerves and brain tissue. Avoid King Mackerel, though, which can have high mercury levels.

beef & cauliflower

Organic beef is more expensive than conventional because it is a much higher-quality product. It's better to eat beef less frequently and eat it organically than to eat cheap conventional meat more often.

MAKES:
4 servings

PREPARATION TIME:
5 minutes

COOKING TIME:
15 minutes

STORAGE:
Refrigerate up to 2 days or freeze cubes of the cooled puree up to 1 month.

¼ cup 1in. cauliflower florets
1 tsp. olive oil
3oz. lean ground beef

1 Put the cauliflower in a steamer and steam, covered, over boiling water 15 minutes, or until completely soft. Reserve the steam water. Meanwhile, heat a small skillet over medium heat. Add the olive oil and when it is hot, add the ground beef. Cook 10 minutes, stirring occasionally, or until thoroughly cooked through. If using a blender with a plastic container, leave both the beef and cauliflower to cool completely before blending.

2 Transfer the beef and cauliflower to a blender. Blend 1 minute, slowly adding a little of the steam water 1 tablespoon at a time, until smooth. Serve warm, reheating if necessary.

beef that is organic and grass-fed is low in fat and a great source of B vitamins. It's also rich in zinc, which is essential for normal growth, the immune system, and appetite control.

venison & parsnip

Wild meats offer another healthy alternative to intensively farmed meats. Venison's strong, earthy flavor is nicely balanced here by the parsnip.

MAKES:
4 servings

PREPARATION TIME:
5 minutes

COOKING TIME:
15 minutes

STORAGE:
Refrigerate up to 2 days or freeze cubes of the cooled puree up to 1 month.

⅓ cup parsnip cut into ¼in. slices
2 tsp. olive oil
3oz. venison

1 Put the parsnip in a steamer and steam, covered, over boiling water 15 minutes, or until completely soft. Reserve the steam water.

2 Meanwhile, heat a small skillet over medium heat. Add the olive oil and when it is hot, add the venison. Cook, partially covered, 5 minutes, or until beginning to brown. Turn it over and cook, partially covered, 5 minutes longer, or until thoroughly cooked through. If using a blender with a plastic container, leave both the venison and parsnip to cool completely before blending.

3 Transfer the venison and parsnip to a blender. Blend 1 minute, slowly adding a little of the steam water 1 tablespoon at a time, until smooth. Serve warm, reheating if necessary.

chicken & zucchini ▾

This delicious dish is sure to be a hit. Use organic chicken, especially for a baby. It is superior in quality, texture, and taste and won't contain antibiotic residues.

MAKES:
4 servings

PREPARATION TIME:
5 minutes

COOKING TIME:
10 minutes

STORAGE:
Refrigerate up to 2 days or freeze cubes of the cooled puree up to 1 month.

2 tsp. olive oil
1 small boneless, skinless chicken breast half, about 3½oz., coarsely chopped
½ zucchini, quartered lengthwise and cut into ¼in.-thick pieces

1 Heat a small skillet over medium heat. Add the olive oil and when it is hot, add the chicken and zucchini. Cook, covered, 10 minutes, stirring occasionally, until the zucchini is soft and the chicken is cooked through and the juices run clear. If using a blender with a plastic container, leave the mixture to cool completely before blending.

2 Transfer the chicken and zucchini to a blender and blend 2 to 3 minutes until smooth, adding a little water if necessary. Serve warm, reheating if necessary.

Lumps to solids

Your baby's appetite is really growing! She's now getting the majority of her calories from food, rather than breast milk or formula, so it's more important than ever to optimize her daily nutrition. Seeded fruit, such as kiwi and raspberries, are a great addition to her diet. Probiotic plain yogurt is no longer just for soaking —she can eat it now on its own or mixed into her food. At this age, she's certainly ready to put her new teeth to use on more textured foods, too. This means you can gradually start phasing out the purees and giving her little bits of food instead. Remember variety is key in helping your baby to develop a love of good food. Buttery Grits, colorful Saucy Steam-Fry, and flavorful Broiled Onion Chicken are just some of the delicious new options she's ready to devour.

Rutabaga & Bok Choy (see page 65)

9 to 12 months

The amount of food your baby is eating now can be quite impressive. Feel free to continue mixing and matching your frozen food cubes from chapters 1 and 2 in addition to trying the new recipes in this chapter. A good ratio to follow at this age is one part starch to one part vegetable, plus good seed oil and some protein. Add extra nutrition to your child's meals wherever you can. For example, sprinkle her beans and grains with finely chopped herbs, such as parsley or basil.

FATS: Good fats continue to be important, so keep giving your child two teaspoons cold-pressed seed oil once each day. Carry on with other nutritious sources of essential fats as well, such as avocado and oily fish.

YOGURT & KEFIR: Carry on with breast milk or formula. I have always let my babies take as much breast milk as they like because it is such an excellent food, and by this stage they are naturally taking less. I offer it away from solid food, though, so it doesn't fill them up before they eat. If you're using formula, follow the directions on the package to determine how much to give your baby at this age. You can also introduce probiotic, organic plain yogurt and kefir—both are good sources of calcium and protein, and they contain important bacteria that support good digestive health. Your baby's digestive system is still developing, though, so I recommend waiting a few more months before introducing other dairy products (see page 90).

TEXTURE IN FOOD: At this age, most children will be able to handle more texture in their food. You may be able to stop pureeing meals altogether, or you may have to puree them only a little. If she wasn't interested in finely grated or small pieces of raw fruits and vegetables before, she should be able to eat them now. As your baby's motor skills develop, finger foods will become more interesting to her, and she might be able to manage some pieces of peach, grapes, or cucumber, peeled and deseeded. Cut fruit or vegetables into ¼-inch pieces to avoid choking and always sit with your child while she eats in case she needs your help. You can also add in fruit with little seeds now, such as kiwi and blackberries. Don't worry if your baby isn't chewing much yet and still needs a lot of things pureed. She'll get there soon.

OATS: Even though I don't introduce other grains that contain gluten until one year, I do introduce oats at nine months. They are a low-gluten grain, which makes them a good first choice to see how your child will handle the proteins in gluten. Use oats sparingly at first as she approaches one year. Unsalted rice cakes are still great when she's teething, but you can try introducing unsalted oatcakes as well (be careful of choking). Or, try the

Berry Oatmeal on page 58 for breakfast. Watch for any reaction in your baby. If she does react, wait eight weeks and then try again.

SPROUTS: You can introduce sprouts now, too. Sprouts are considered "live foods" because the seeds are germinating and growing. The nutrition in live food is far superior to other foods. The living enzymes in the sprouts aid our digestion and our assimilation of nutrients. This also makes them very easy to digest. Toss them in the blender when you puree your baby's meal or chop them and mix them into her food. You really can't overuse them, and you're adding a phenomenal course of nutrition.

NEW FOODS TO INTRODUCE AT 9 TO 12 MONTHS

Your child is now ready for the foods listed in the chart below. Combine them with the foods listed in the previous chapters to give her the best variety you can.

FRUIT	VEGETABLES	GRAINS	FISH*	DAIRY & EGGS	FATS
• blackberry	• asparagus	• corn	* Avoid overfished varieties, such as cod	• kefir	• butter
• blueberry	• bok choy	• oat		• yogurt	
• cranberry (fresh or unsweetened dried)	• Chinese cabbage				
	• cucumber				
	• fennel		• haddock		
• currant	• garlic		• pollock		
• date	• fresh herbs, such as basil, mint, and parsley		• trout		
• fig					
• grape	• Jerusalem artichoke				
• kiwi					
• lychee	• onion				
• raisin	• scallion				
• raspberry	• sprouts (all types, including alfalfa, broccoli, chickpea, and lentil)				
• rhubarb					

With my kids, I found I had a feeding window. If I didn't get all the food in their mouths within twenty minutes—thirty minutes tops—they would lose interest or the little bit of food they had eaten would hit their stomach and make them feel full. So, try to get the meal in as quickly as is comfortable. I also found my kids got restless after a short while, so I always had little toys on the table to keep them busy at this age. If they're happy at the table, you can keep putting food in their mouths. When the kids are older and feeding themselves, I don't allow toys, but at this age they can be a huge help.

EATING ON THE GO: You'll be out and about a lot now, and taking snacks or food with you is easy. A little container of cut-up fruit or a banana is a great portable snack that your baby can eat in her stroller or in a high chair when you go out. It'll keep her busy and give you a chance to relax with a friend over a cup of coffee. Many of the meals in this and the previous chapters are portable, too. Fish and meat dishes require refrigeration, though, so save them for meals at home. Instead, take a container of grain mixed with bean or vegetables if you're going to be out for a couple of hours. Just remember to bring a bib, spoon, bottle of filtered water, and some paper towels or wipes.

Meals for Yourself

You're doing a lot of cooking for your baby right now. You might be buying lots of new ingredients you haven't traditionally used, and your refrigerator might be full of food with which you're not that familiar. Remember these foods aren't just for children. You can do a lot to boost your own energy and overall sense of well-being right now by making sure you eat just as healthily as your baby. Instead of letting ingredients spoil and get thrown away, make a quick supper for yourself and your partner. If you're tired at the end of the day and have no idea what the two of you should eat, cook some pasta, steam some of the vegetables you've got, throw on some seeds, drizzle with olive oil—and relax. It doesn't need to be a big production to be satisfying, nutritious, and delicious.

Avoiding Waste

Now that your refrigerator is full of great new ingredients, try to use things quickly so they don't spoil. It's a shame to throw away good food just because you forgot about it or didn't have time to cook. One way to avoid this is to make sure you're storing foods properly. Each recipe in this book includes storage instructions that will let you know if a food is suitable to be frozen or refrigerated.

Air makes food stale, so always remember to put leftover foods and perishables such as crackers, grains, cookies, and rice cakes in airtight containers so that they will stay fresh longer.

MEAL PLANNER FOR BABIES AT 9 TO 12 MONTHS

This meal planner uses all the recipes in this chapter over the course of a week.
Even if you make only the majority, you and your baby will be doing really well.

DAY	BREAKFAST	MID-MORNING	LUNCH	MID-AFTERNOON	DINNER	EVENING
1	Gluten-Free Oatmeal with Dates (see page 59) with 2 tsp. seed oil	breast/bottle	Brown Rice & Sprouts (see page 65) sweet potato puree (see Carrot Puree on page 29) warm water	breast/bottle	Pollock with Green Beans (see page 68) with 2 tsp. olive oil warm water	breast/bottle
2	rice puffs with yogurt	breast/bottle	Jerusalem Artichoke & Onion Simmer (see page 64) Carrot Puree (see page 29) warm water	breast/bottle	Rutabaga & Bok Choy (see page 65) Quinoa Puree (see page 33) with 2 tsp. seed oil warm water	breast/bottle
3	Berry Oatmeal (see page 58) with 2 tsp. seed oil	breast/bottle	Cannellini Beans & Amaranth (see page 64) Butternut Squash Puree (see page 30) warm water	breast/bottle	Broiled Onion Chicken (see page 67) with 2 tsp. olive oil Broccoli & Cauliflower Puree (see page 29) warm water	breast/bottle
4	cornflakes (no added sugar) with rice milk	breast/bottle	Buttered Turnip Sauté (see page 61) beet puree (see Butternut Squash Puree on page 30) with 2 tsp. olive oil warm water	breast/bottle	Quinoa, Chinese Leaves & Carrot Stew (see page 61) with 2 tsp. seed oil warm water	breast/bottle
5	Fruit Ambrosia (see page 60) unsalted oatcakes	breast/bottle	Saucy Steam-Fry (see page 62) Amaranth Puree (see page 32) with 2 tsp. seed oil warm water	breast/bottle	Beef & Cauliflower (see page 50) with 2 tsp. olive oil Snow Peas, Cucumber & Yogurt Salad (see page 67) warm water	breast/bottle
6	Millet Puree (see page 33) mango puree (see Apple Puree on page 26)	breast/bottle	Avocado Mash (see page 28) with millet flakes and yogurt warm water	breast/bottle	Baby Brown Rice Puree (see page 30) pumpkin puree (see Butternut Squash Puree on page 30) with 2 tsp. seed oil warm water	breast/bottle
7	Grits (see page 59)	breast/bottle	Red Lentil Puree (see page 34) Quinoa Puree (see page 33) steamed carrot warm water	breast/bottle	Sardines & Sweet Potato (see page 49) grated raw rutabaga warm water	breast/bottle

▲ berry oatmeal

MAKES:
4 servings

PREPARATION TIME:
5 minutes, plus overnight soaking

COOKING TIME:
10 minutes

STORAGE:
Refrigerate up to 3 days or freeze up to 3 months.

The sweet, tart berries featured in this delicious version of oatmeal will be a great flavor experience for your baby, but you can use any mixture of stewed or fresh fruit. (From 15 months you can add ground seeds and/or nuts, too.)

1 cup rolled oats
1 tbsp. kefir or plain yogurt
1 cup plain yogurt
1 cup berries, such as raspberries, blueberries, or blackberries

1 Put the oats and 1 tablespoon kefir in a small saucepan. Add 3 cups water and leave to soak, covered, overnight at room temperature.

2 Bring the soaked oats to a simmer over medium heat, then reduce the heat to low and cook, stirring occasionally, 10 minutes, or until soft and creamy. Remove from the heat.

3 Mix in the 1 cup yogurt and berries. If the mixture is too coarse, transfer it to a blender and blend 1 minute until smooth. If using a blender with a plastic container, leave the porridge to cool completely before blending. Serve warm, reheating if necessary.

gluten-free "oatmeal" with dates

MAKES:
4 servings

PREPARATION
TIME:
5 minutes

COOKING TIME:
15 minutes

STORAGE:
Refrigerate
up to 3 days
or freeze up
to 3 months.

This easy and delicious oatmeal-style cereal uses three gluten-free grains. It's one of my favorite creations, and Jessie, Nicholas, and Cassie love it.

3 tbsp. millet flakes
3 tbsp. quinoa flakes
3 tbsp. buckwheat flakes
3 tbsp. chopped dried
   dates

1 Put all the ingredients and 2 cups water in a medium saucepan. Bring to a simmer over medium heat, then reduce the heat to low and cook 15 minutes, stirring continuously, or until soft. Remove from the heat and leave to cool a little. Serve warm.

2 If a smoother consistency is desired, transfer the mixture to a blender (leaving it to cool completely first if using a blender with a plastic container) and blend for 1 minute until smooth. Serve warm, reheating if necessary.

grits

SERVES:
2 adults and
2 children

PREPARATION
TIME:
5 minutes

COOKING TIME:
20 minutes

STORAGE:
Not suitable
for storage.

Grits are a traditional corn dish from the southern states. This gorgeous, buttery dish makes a fabulous breakfast the entire family will enjoy. You can also serve it as a side dish—in the South, it's often eaten with pork. (Once your baby has reached one year, you can stir in ¾ teaspoon salt in step 1 for extra flavor.)

1½ cups coarsely ground
   cornmeal (hominy
   grits)
1½ sticks (12 tbsp.) butter,
   cut into 6 pieces

cornmeal
is great for a healthy heart. It contain lots of folate, a B vitamin that helps lower levels of homocysteine, an amino acid that can be dangerous at high levels.

1 In a medium saucepan, bring 6 cups water to a boil. Add the cornmeal and whisk quickly with a wire whisk until the mixture is smooth, without any lumps. Reduce the heat to medium-low and simmer 20 minutes, stirring with the whisk every few minutes, or until thick.

2 Remove from the heat and divide into four bowls. Top each child portion with 1 piece of the butter and each adult portion with 2 pieces. Serve hot.

▼ fruit ambrosia

MAKES:
2 servings

PREPARATION TIME:
10 minutes

STORAGE:
Refrigerate up to 1 day.

You can serve this versatile recipe with cooked grains instead of millet flakes, if you prefer. It makes a fabulous base for smoothies, too: just omit the millet flakes and add any other fruit from this or previous chapters to create a great mid-morning or mid-afternoon drink snack.

1 banana, peeled
2oz. seedless red grapes
1 kiwi, peeled and
  roughly chopped
4 tbsp. Greek-style yogurt
  or thick plain yogurt
4 tbsp. instant millet
  flakes

1 Put the banana, grapes, kiwi, and yogurt in a blender and pulse a few times until lumpy.

2 Divide the mixture into two bowls, then stir 2 tablespoons of the millet flakes into each portion and serve.

yogurt
is a health-promoting wonderfood that gives your baby good bacteria, protein, calcium, vitamin B12, and other nutrients. Offer it plain or mixed with cereals, nuts, and fruit.

buttered turnip sauté

Your little one won't be able to get enough of these succulent, buttery turnips. A versatile, often overlooked vegetable, turnips are great raw, too. Try serving them finely grated into salads.

MAKES:
4 servings

PREPARATION TIME:
10 minutes

COOKING TIME:
10 minutes

STORAGE:
Refrigerate up to 3 days or freeze cubes of the mixture up to 3 months.

2 tbsp. butter
1 cup quartered turnips cut into ¼in.-thick slices

1 Melt the butter in a large skillet over low heat. Add the turnips and cook 10 minutes, or until completely soft. Stir occasionally to ensure they cook evenly.

2 Mash the turnips, using a fork, and serve warm. If a smoother consistency is desired, transfer to a blender (leaving it to cool completely first if using a blender with a plastic container) and blend for 1 minute until smooth. Serve warm, reheating if necessary.

quinoa, chinese cabbage & carrot stew

This colorful stew makes a quick, delicious meal. Chinese cabbage is great —it can also be used finely chopped in salads and on sandwiches.

MAKES:
4 servings

PREPARATION TIME:
10 minutes

COOKING TIME:
35 minutes

STORAGE:
Refrigerate up to 3 days or freeze cubes of the stew up to 3 months.

⅓ cup quinoa
1 carrot, cut into ½in.-thick slices
2 heads of Chinese cabbage, about 4oz., cut into ½in. squares

quinoa **is a complete protein This means it contains all the essential amino acids your child needs, including cystine, lysine, and methionine —amino acids that are low in other grains.**

1 Put the quinoa in a strainer and rinse under cold running water, then drain well. Transfer to a medium saucepan and toast over high heat minutes, stirring continuously, until any excess water evaporates and the quinoa is light brown and beginning to pop.

2 Slowly add 2 cups water and bring to a boil over high heat. Reduce the heat to low and simmer, covered, 10 minutes. Add the carrots and simmer, covered, 10 minutes longer, then add the cabbage. Continue simmering, covered, an additional 10 minutes, or until the grain and vegetables are very soft. If using a blender with a plastic container, leave the mixture to cool completely before blending.

3 Transfer the mixture to a blender and blend 1 minute, or until the desired consistency is achieved. Serve warm, reheating if necessary.

saucy steam-fry

MAKES:
4 servings

PREPARATION TIME:
15 minutes

COOKING TIME:
20 minutes

STORAGE:
Refrigerate up to 3 days.

The visual impact of food is important for children. They love bright colors, and this dish is bursting with them. The orange, white, and green vegetables cut into pretty little shapes are sure to catch your baby's eye and get her excited about this meal.

2 tsp. kuzu
1 tbsp. toasted sesame oil
1 carrot, quartered lengthways and cut into ¼in.-thick slices
⅓ cup ½in. cauliflower florets
⅓ cup ½in. broccoli florets
1 tsp. mirin
1 cup dried corn pasta
salt

1 In a small bowl, mix together the kuzu and 1 tablespoon cold water, stirring until the kuzu dissolves, then set aside.

2 Heat a wok or large skillet over medium-low heat. Add the sesame oil, carrot, and 4 tablespoons hot water. Steam-fry, stirring frequently, 5 minutes. As the pan begins to dry out, add another 4 tablespoons hot water. Cook 5 minutes longer, or until the carrot begins to soften. Meanwhile, bring a large pan of salted water to a boil and cook the pasta 2 minutes longer than the package directions so it is very soft, then drain.

3 Add the cauliflower and another 4 tablespoons hot water to the wok and steam-fry 3 minutes longer, stirring frequently, until the cauliflower begins to become soft. Add the broccoli and another 4 tablespoons hot water and continue steam-frying, stirring occasionally, 5 minutes longer.

4 Stir the kuzu mixture and mirin into the vegetables and cook, stirring, 2 minutes, or until the vegetables are tender and the sauce is thick and shimmery. Remove from the heat.

5 Divide the pasta into four bowls and top each portion with one-quarter of the steam-fry. Serve warm. If a smoother consistency is desired, transfer the pasta and vegetables to a blender (leaving them to cool completely first if using a blender with a plastic container) and pulse a few times until lumpy. If using a blender with a plastic container, leave the pasta and vegetables to cool completely before blending. Serve warm, reheating if necessary.

kuzu
is an outstanding gelling and thickening agent that also has soothing medicinal effects. It can relieve digestive problems, and its high flavanoid content aids circulation by helping to dilate blood vessels.

cannellini beans & amaranth

MAKES:
4 servings

PREPARATION TIME:
5 minutes, plus overnight soaking and making the amaranth puree

COOKING TIME:
1 hour 40 minutes

STORAGE:
Refrigerate up to 3 days or freeze cubes of the puree up to 3 months.

Combining creamy cannellini beans with subtly sweet amaranth makes a delicious protein-rich meal.

½ cup dried cannellini beans
2 tsp. lemon juice
1 strip of kombu, about 3¼ x 2in., cut into little pieces
4 portions Amaranth Puree (see page 34)

1 Put the beans and lemon juice in a medium saucepan, cover with water, and leave to soak, covered, overnight.

2 Drain and rinse the beans. Return them to the pan and add 2¼ cups water. Bring to a boil over high heat and boil 10 minutes, skimming any scum that rises to the surface. Reduce the heat to low, add the kombu, and cook, covered, 1½ hours, or until the beans are completely soft, then discard the kombu.

3 Mash the beans with a fork, then mix with an equal portion of the amaranth puree and serve warm. If a smoother consistency is desired, transfer the mixture to a blender (leaving it to cool completely first if using a blender with a plastic container). Pulse 1 minute, or until the desired consistency is achieved. Serve warm, reheating if necessary.

jerusalem artichoke & onion simmer

MAKES:
8 servings

PREPARATION TIME:
10 minutes

COOKING TIME:
30 minutes

STORAGE:
Refrigerate up to 3 days or freeze cubes of the mixture up to 3 months.

Jerusalem artichokes are a bit like potatoes with a hint of artichoke flavor. The hotter the raw onion, the sweeter it is when cooked, so if you're crying while you're chopping, your kids will probably love this.

1 tbsp. olive oil
2 cups trimmed and sliced Jerusalem artichokes
1 small onion, finely chopped

1 Heat a large saucepan over medium-low heat and add the oil. When it is hot, add the artichokes, onion and enough water to just cover the vegetables. Simmer, covered, 30 minutes, stirring occasionally and adding a little water if the vegetables start to dry out.

2 Mash with a fork and serve warm. If a smoother consistency is desired, transfer the mixture to a blender (leaving it to cool completely first if using a blender with a plastic container) and blend 1 minute, or until the desired consistency is achieved. Serve warm, reheating if necessary.

rutabaga & bok choy

A beautiful dish, the green bok choy creates visual appeal, while its clean, fresh flavor brightens up the more somber rutabaga.

MAKES:
4 servings

PREPARATION TIME:
10 minutes

COOKING TIME:
25 minutes

STORAGE:
Refrigerate up to 3 days or freeze cubes of the mixture up to 3 months.

3 cups peeled rutabaga cut into ½in. cubes
½ cup bok choy cut into ½in.-wide strips

1 Put the rutabaga in a steamer and steam, covered, over boiling water 20 minutes, or until completely soft, then remove from the steamer and set aside. Reserve the steam water.

2 Put the bok choy in the steamer and steam, covered, over boiling water 3 minutes, or until wilted. Reserve the steam water. If using a blender with a plastic container, leave the vegetables to cool completely before blending.

3 Transfer the vegetables to the blender and pulse 1 minute, or until the mixture forms a lumpy puree, slowly adding a little of the steam water, if necessary. If a smoother consistency is desired, blend for a little longer. Serve warm, reheating if necessary.

brown rice & sprouts

One of Nicholas's favorites, this dish is brilliant on its own or as a base into which you can mix other foods. Using sprouted seeds is a lovely way to add vitality to your growing child's diet.

MAKES:
4 servings

PREPARATION TIME:
5 minutes, plus at least 7 hours soaking

COOKING TIME:
1 hour

STORAGE:
Refrigerate up to 2 days or freeze cubes the mixture up to 1 month. Reheat until hot.

½ cup short-grain brown rice
1 tbsp. kefir or plain yogurt
1 garlic clove, crushed
2oz. alfalfa sprouts

1 Put the rice, kefir, and 2½ cups warm water in a medium saucepan and leave to soak, covered, 7 hours, or overnight.

2 Add the garlic to the rice and bring to a boil over high heat, then reduce the heat to low and simmer, covered, 1 hour, or until the rice is very tender. If using a blender with a plastic container, leave the mixture to cool completely before blending.

3 Transfer the mixture to a blender, add the sprouts, and blend 1 minute, or until smooth. Serve warm, reheating if necessary.

sprouts are one of the most complex, nutritional foods. They're rich in vitamins, minerals, and proteins. What really sets these "live foods" apart are their enzymes, which boost the digestive system.

◀ snow peas, cucumber & yogurt salad

Fresh vegetables mixed with yogurt make a delicious first salad for your little one—and this combination was a big hit with Jessie. For variation, add chopped cucumber and avocado. (From one year, you can add chopped tomato, too.)

MAKES:
1 serving

PREPARATION TIME:
10 minutes

COOKING TIME:
10 minutes

STORAGE:
Not suitable for storage.

4 snow peas, cut into bite-size pieces
1 x 3in. piece cucumber, peeled, seeded and cut into bite-size pieces
1 tsp. plain yogurt

1 Put the snow peas in a steamer and steam, covered, over boiling water 10 minutes, or until soft. Remove from the heat and leave to cool completely.

2 Put the snow peas, cucumber, and yogurt in a small bowl, mix well, and serve. If a smoother consistency is desired, transfer the mixture to a blender and pulse a few times until the desired consistency is achieved, then serve.

broiled onion chicken

Broiling brings out great flavors in the onion and the chicken. Use organic chicken and you get meat with less water and more flavor.

MAKES:
2 servings

PREPARATION TIME:
5 minutes

COOKING TIME:
11 minutes

STORAGE:
Refrigerate up to 2 days or freeze cubes of the mixture up to 1 month.

1 tsp. olive oil
⅓ cup boneless, skinless chicken breast half cut into small chunks
1 small onion, finely chopped

1 Preheat the broiler to medium and grease a medium, shallow baking pan with the oil. Put the chicken and onion in the baking pan and broil 6 to 7 minutes until the onion and chicken begin to brown.

2 Remove from the broiler, stir and then broil 3 to 4 minutes longer until the chicken is cooked through and the juices run clear. Serve warm.

3 If a smoother consistency is desired, transfer the chicken and onion to a blender (leaving it to cool completely first if using a blender with a plastic container). Pulse 1 minute, or until the desired consistency is achieved, then serve warm, reheating if necessary.

pollock with green beans

Pollock is mild, lean, tender fish. The fillets are usually bone-free with a consistent snow-white color. It flakes easily, making it perfect for kids —and it's a great alternative to overfished cod.

MAKES:
4 servings

PREPARATION
TIME:
10 minutes

COOKING TIME:
15 minutes

STORAGE:
Refrigerate the
fish up to 2 days
or freeze in cubes
up to 1 month.
Refrigerate the
beans up to 3 days
or freeze in cubes
up to 3 months.

½ cup green beans
   trimmed and cut into
   1in.-long pieces
1½ tsp. olive oil
3½oz. pollock fillet, rinsed

1 Put the green beans in a steamer and steam, covered, over boiling water 15 minutes, until completely soft.

2 While the beans are steaming, heat a small skillet over medium heat. Add ½ teaspoon of the olive oil and when it is hot, add the pollock, skin-side up. Cook, covered, 5 minutes, then turn the fish over and cook, covered, 5 to 10 minutes longer until white and cooked through. Remove from the heat, then remove and discard the skin.

3 Cut the fish roughly, checking with your fingers for bones, then transfer to a bowl and mash with a fork. If a smoother consistency is desired, transfer the fish to a blender and blend 1 minute until smooth. If using a blender with a plastic container, leave the fish and beans to cool completely before blending.

4 Transfer the beans to a clean blender, add the remaining olive oil, and pulse 1 minute, or until the mixture forms a lumpy puree. Serve warm with the fish, reheating if necessary.

white fish
is the best source of low-fat animal protein. Protein is vital for a strong immune system and the development of healthy bones, skin, nails, and hair. Packed with vitamins and minerals, white fish also provides metabolism-boosting iodine and B vitamins.

eating more

Between his first birthday and the time he turns two, your baby will reach some remarkable developmental milestones. If he hasn't already taken his first steps, he will very soon. Before you know it, he'll be off and running—with you in quick pursuit. In the coming months, he'll start talking and acquiring lots of new motor skills as well. All of this growth and energy requires fuel, and the best fuel you can continue to give him is a nutrition-packed diet. He's now ready for some great new foods, such as potatoes, tomatoes, eggs, and whole grains like barley, rye, and spelt. From 15 months, he can also have seeds, nuts, and wheat. With delicious options like Spelt French Toast, Best Hamburgers, Quesadillas, and Tuna Pie, mealtimes are about to become significantly more exciting.

Quesadillas (see page 101)

12 to 15 months

With such a huge variety of foods and ingredients in your baby's diet now, it's easy to provide him with a wonderful mix of tastes, textures, and nutrients. Whether or not you continue breastfeeding is a very personal decision and will be influenced by many factors. If you can or want to, carry on with breast milk or formula. Your baby will naturally take much less milk now because the majority of his nutrition is coming from food. By one year, my babies and I had settled into a comfortable feeding schedule. I found there were two times in the day, once in the morning and once at night, when I liked to breastfeed. As a working mother, this made sense for me, but if you find that a different schedule suits you better, go with that.

WEANING OFF BREAST MILK: If you wean your baby off breast milk or formula now, I don't recommend replacing it with cow's milk (see page 13). You can rely on yogurt and a wide variety of foods for calcium and magnesium, or you can offer organic goat or sheep's milk if you really want to. If you do use cow's milk, buy organic milk—it not only excludes hormone residues and antibiotic residues, it also offers more nutrition.

CHEWING: If your baby is still not chewing a lot, simply continue with mushy or lumpy purees for now to ensure he is getting a good quantity of food, and continue encouraging him with finger foods like rice cakes and small pieces of raw fruit and vegetables. You might find some of the recipes in this chapter, such as Fried Egg on Rye and Best Beef Burgers, will have to wait until he has mastered the art of chewing. If that's the case, just try some of the softer foods, such as Cornbread Pudding and Mashed Potato Craters, and continue with the recipes from the previous chapters. The rest can wait until later. Again, there is no rush. And if there's any doubt, it's better to go with softer food anyway so you know he's properly digesting and assimilating what he eats.

EGGS: You can offer eggs now, which are an excellent source of protein. Some people worry about salmonella, but I don't get overly worried about foods being dangerous. After three kids and lots and lots of eggs, I have never had a problem. Just make sure you buy organic eggs, which are produced in less-crowded conditions, where disease does not spread as easily as in conventional farming. I don't like to overcook eggs, but for this age, I tend to scramble or fry them with the yolk broken so I can see they are thoroughly cooked.

SOY: You can also offer soy from one year old, but I recommend keeping the quantity to a minimum for both children and adults. Soy contains phytoestrogens, which can disrupt the body's hormone balance. As I mentioned earlier, in countries where soy and its products are traditionally eaten, they are consumed only in small amounts and not as a protein substitute. Tofu is fine once in a while, but tempeh is better because it is fermented, contains valuable B vitamins and is easier to digest.

NIGHTSHADES: Your baby is now ready to eat eggplant, potato, and tomato. Although these are very common foods, I wait to introduce them until after one year because they belong to the nightshade family of vegetables. This means they contain a particular group of substances, called alkaloids, which can impact on nerve-muscle function and digestive function, and can also compromise joint function. These foods

NEW FOODS TO INTRODUCE AT 12 TO 15 MONTHS

Your child is now ready for the foods listed in the chart below. Combine them with the foods listed in the previous chapters to give him the best variety you can.

FRUIT	VEGETABLES	GRAINS	LEGUMES	DAIRY & EGGS
• citrus (in small amounts): clementine kumquat lemon lime mandarin pomelo satsuma tangelo tangerine No orange or grapefruit • passion fruit • pomegranate • strawberry	• arugula • cabbage • caper • chard • corn • eggplant • gherkin • green bell pepper • kale • lettuce • mushroom • olives (pitted) • potato • spinach • sweet bell pepper (red, yellow, orange, etc.) • tomato • watercress	• barley • Kamut • rye • spelt	• soy (keep to a minimum), including tempeh and tofu	• eggs

do have nutritional benefits; it's just a good idea not to become too dependent on them. As you know by now, there are so many other foods to enjoy.

SPINACH: Spinach is an easy vegetable to overuse, and it can sometimes be difficult to digest, so I wait until one year to introduce it. By then, your baby's digestive system is mature enough to handle it.

MUSHROOMS: I also wait until one year to introduce mushrooms. Although they're very nutritious, they contain a high percentage of chitin, a polysaccharide that is difficult to digest. Cooking is essential to break down the chitinous cell walls. As with other foods in earlier chapters, if your child gets an upset tummy or other reaction after eating them, give him a bit more time and try again in six to eight weeks.

SOUPS: When your child is very young and first adjusting to food, it's important he doesn't fill up with watery meals. Now that he's eating more solid food and getting much less breast milk or formula (if any), you can introduce soups. They're a good way to incorporate grains, legumes, and vegetables into his diet. The soups in this chapter are substantial enough to make a meal, especially when served with some kind of protein.

GLUTEN: At one year, your baby's digestive system should be mature enough to handle most gluten, so you can begin to offer pastas. Look for wholegrain spelt or Kamut pasta and alternate them with gluten-free alternatives, such as buckwheat noodles and corn pasta. I suggest cooking pasta for a couple of minutes longer than recommended on the package so it's soft, which will allow your baby to easily chew and digest it. If you've been eating white pasta and make the switch to wholegrain pastas when you introduce them to your baby, I think you'll be delighted with the lovely flavor and texture the whole grains give this familiar food. Note, however, that although grains containing gluten are fine for a one-year-old child, I do not introduce wheat until fifteen months. This is because grains such as spelt are better nutritionally, and it's much too easy to consume too much wheat. Let your child experience these other grains and get used to them before trying wheat.

BREADS & CRACKERS: It's also great to be able to offer your child bread and crackers made from spelt, Kamut, barley, or rye. They make convenient, portable snacks and are a good carrier for spreads like hummus and seed butters. To relieve teething discomfort, you can give him grissini, crispbreads, and crackers made from these grains, too.

Breads and crackers are easy to get a hold of, but make sure you don't give up all the great habits and other foods you have been using until now. Keep giving him different grains, such as brown rice, millet, and quinoa—if he's chewing well, you won't even have to puree them any more. Raw vegetables, cut into sticks or slices, and fresh or dried fruit are still good for snacking on. Make sure your baby continues to get a good range of foods with lots of variation in flavors, textures, and colors.

MEAL PLANNER FOR TODDLERS AT 12 TO 15 MONTHS

Don't be daunted by how many recipes there are on this meal planner. Follow it as closely as is comfortable, and make and freeze batches whenever possible.

DAY	BREAKFAST	MID-MORNING	LUNCH	MID-AFTERNOON	DINNER
1	Mustard Scrambled Eggs (see page 78) rye toast	fruit (fresh or dried)	Tomato Soup with Rice (see page 81) with 2 tsp. seed oil nori squares	corn cakes	Chicken & Mushroom Pasta (see page 88) raw peas
2	cornflakes (no added sugar) with yogurt	fruit (fresh or dried)	Fried Egg on Rye (see page 78) celery sticks	oatcakes	Baked Beans with Baked Potatoes (see page 83) grated cheddar cheese steamed broccoli with 2 tsp. seed oil
3	Wholegrain Spelt Pancakes (see page 76)	fruit (fresh or dried)	Millet Puree (see page 33) sweet potato puree (see Carrot Puree on page 29) with 2 tsp. olive oil	low-salt/baked tortillas	Best Beef Burgers (see page 88) steamed carrot with 2 tsp. seed oil
4	Cornbread Pudding (see page 79)	fruit (fresh or dried)	Squash & Potato Soup (see page 80) with 2 tsp. olive oil steamed snow peas	low-salt popcorn	Amaranth Puree (see page 32) with sprouts and 2 tsp. seed oil smoked salmon sweet pepper
5	Spelt French Toast (see page 79)	fruit (fresh or dried)	Creamy Rustic Soup (see page 82) with 2 tsp. seed oil	Japanese rice crackers	Cherry Tomato Spaghetti (see page 84) steamed cauliflower
6	Gluten-Free Oatmeal with Dates (see page 59) with 2 tsp. seed oil	fruit (fresh or dried)	Mashed Potato Craters (see page 84) olives steamed zucchini	wholewheat grissini or pretzels	Wholegrain Risotto with Asparagus (see page 87) broiled fish grated beet with 2 tsp. seed oil
7	seed- and nut-free muesli with rice milk	fruit (fresh or dried)	Pollock with Green Beans (see page 68) with 2 tsp. olive oil wholegrain spelt toast	wholegrain rye crackers/crispbreads	Saucy Steam-Fry (see page 62) chopped arugula with 2 tsp. seed oil

wholegrain spelt pancakes

Transform the relatively unhealthy breakfast of white-flour pancakes into a nutritious—and delicious—meal by using wholegrain spelt flour. Pancakes travel well and make a great snack for a hungry toddler.

SERVES:
2 adults and
2 children

PREPARATION
TIME:
10 minutes

COOKING TIME:
30 minutes

STORAGE:
Refrigerate the uncooked batter up to 2 days. Refrigerate the cooked pancakes up to 3 days.

2¾ cups wholegrain spelt flour
1 tbsp. baking powder
½ tsp. salt
1 egg, beaten
1½ cups rice milk, plus extra as needed
2 tbsp. olive oil, plus extra for frying
½ cup blueberries, chopped strawberries, or chopped banana (optional)

To serve:
butter
maple syrup
½ lemon, cut into wedges
sugar

1 Preheat the oven to 150°F. In a small bowl, mix together the flour, baking powder, and salt. In a medium bowl, whisk together the egg, rice milk, and olive oil. Pour the dry mixture into the wet ingredients and whisk until smooth. Using a wooden spoon or rubber spatula, fold in the blueberries, if using.

2 Heat a griddle over medium-low heat until hot or heat a little olive oil in a large skillet. For each pancake, drop 1 to 2 tablespoonfuls of the batter onto the hot griddle. The pancakes will spread to about 2 inches wide, so space them slightly apart. If the batter is too thick and the pancakes don't spread, add a little more rice milk 1 tablespoon at a time to thin out the batter. Cook 2 minutes, or until the bubbles that appear on the surface pop and the undersides of the pancakes are light brown.

3 Flip the pancakes over. If they stick to the griddle, they are not ready to be turned; leave them to cook a little longer and then flip. Cook the other side of the pancakes 1 to 2 minutes longer until light brown. Transfer to a plate and keep warm in the oven while you make the remaining pancakes. If using a skillet, add more oil to the pan as necessary before each batch.

4 Spread each pancake with a little butter and serve hot drizzled with maple syrup or sprinkled with lemon juice and sugar.

spelt
is an ancient grain related to wheat. It offers a broader spectrum of nutrients than hybridized wheat, and people with sensitivities to wheat can often eat spelt instead.

mustard scrambled eggs

SERVES:
2 adults and
2 children

PREPARATION
TIME:
5 minutes

COOKING TIME:
4 minutes

STORAGE:
Not suitable
for storage.

Protein-packed scrambled eggs are easy for small children to eat. Give your baby a spoon and he should be able to scoop them up from a bowl. The mustard gives them a flavor boost that will spark his interest.

2 tbsp. butter
8 eggs, beaten
¼ tsp. salt
1 tbsp. non-hot mustard

1 Melt the butter in a large skillet over medium-high heat until gently sizzling. Pour the eggs into the pan and sprinkle with the salt. Cook 1 minute, or until the edges of the eggs start to sizzle, then stir with a small wooden spoon 2 to 3 minutes until just cooked. Remove from the heat.

2 Stir in the mustard and serve immediately.

fried egg on rye

SERVES:
2 adults and
2 children

PREPARATION
TIME:
5 minutes

COOKING TIME:
5 minutes

STORAGE:
Not suitable
for storage.

If your baby can chew, this is a good lunch. Nicholas loves how the egg gets a little crunchy when it's fried in the butter, and it's delicious with the toasted rye bread and mayonnaise.

2 tbsp. butter
6 eggs
mayonnaise, to taste, for
    spreading
6 slices of wholegrain rye
    bread

1 Melt the butter in a large skillet over medium-high heat. When it is sizzling hot, break the eggs into the pan one at a time and gently break the yolks. Work in batches, if necessary.

2 Reduce the heat to medium and cook 5 minutes, or until the eggs are just cooked. Meanwhile, toast the bread.

3 Spread some mayonnaise on each slice of bread and top with 1 egg. Serve warm.

spelt french toast

A great breakfast that combines carbs with protein—and a little sweetness. It's hard not to love this dish, no matter how old you are.

SERVES:
2 adults and 2 children

PREPARATION TIME:
5 minutes

COOKING TIME:
20 minutes

STORAGE:
Not suitable for storage.

6 eggs, beaten
3 tbsp. sugar
6 tbsp. rice milk
¼ tsp. vanilla extract
2 tbsp. butter
6 slices of wholegrain spelt bread

1 Preheat the oven to 150°F. Put the eggs, sugar, rice milk, and vanilla extract in a shallow bowl or baking dish and mix well until the sugar dissolves.

2 Melt the butter in a large skillet over medium heat until hot. Put 1 slice of bread in the baking dish and leave to soak in the mixture for a few seconds, then turn it over and soak until moist.

3 Put the soaked bread in the pan, repeat with another slice of bread, and fry 2 to 3 minutes on each side until light brown. Transfer to a plate and keep warm in the oven while you make the rest of the French toast. Serve warm.

cornbread pudding

My grandmother created this delicious breakfast "pudding." It's so good, it's hard to stop eating once you start, especially warm from the oven.

SERVES:
2 adults and 2 children

PREPARATION TIME:
20 minutes

COOKING TIME:
45 minutes

STORAGE:
Refrigerate up to 3 days.

4 tbsp. butter, cubed, plus extra for greasing
1 cup cornmeal
½ cup sugar
1½ cups plus 2 tbsp. rice milk
2 eggs, beaten
1 tsp. gluten-free baking powder
¼ tsp. salt

1 Preheat the oven to 350°F and grease an 8- x 8-inch baking dish with butter. Put the cornmeal in a large mixing bowl and whisk in 2 cups boiling water, using a wire whisk.

2 Add the butter and sugar and mix with a spoon or rubber spatula until smooth and there are not any lumps. Add the rice milk, eggs, baking powder, and salt and mix well. Pour into the baking dish.

3 Bake 45 minutes, or until golden brown and firm at the edges. It will be wobbly in the middle. Remove from the oven and leave to cool 10 minutes, then slice and serve hot, warm, or cold.

rice milk **is an excellent substitute for cow's milk in baking. Made from brown rice, it has a lovely natural sweetness.**

▲ squash & potato soup

This is a quick and easy soup that's perfect on a crisp fall day. Children love the velvety texture, bright color, and gentle sweetness.

SERVES:
2 adults and
2 children

**PREPARATION
TIME:**
15 minutes

COOKING TIME:
30 minutes

STORAGE:
Refrigerate
up to 3 days
or freeze
up to 3 months.

**1 small butternut squash,
    peeled, seeded, and
    diced**
**2 potatoes, unpeeled
    and diced**
2 onions, chopped
**2 garlic cloves, roughly
    chopped**
⅛ tsp. cayenne pepper
2 cups vegetable broth
4 tsp. olive oil

1 Put the squash, potatoes, onions, garlic, cayenne pepper, and vegetable broth in a large saucepan and bring to a boil over medium-high heat. Reduce the heat to medium-low and simmer, covered, 30 minutes, or until the squash and potatoes are soft.

2 Using an immersion blender, puree the mixture 1 to 2 minutes until creamy but still chunky. Add the olive oil and serve hot.

*cayenne
pepper*
**stimulates digestive
juices and is healing to
stomach tissues and other
digestive organs, making
it much gentler on the
body than black
pepper.**

tomato soup with rice

MAKES:
4 servings

PREPARATION
TIME:
20 minutes,
plus at least
7 hours
soaking

COOKING TIME:
1 hour 30 minutes

STORAGE:
Refrigerate the
soup up to 3 days
or freeze
up to 3 months.
Refrigerate the rice
up to 1 day. Reheat
until hot.

There's nothing like homemade tomato soup and, served over rice, it makes a filling meal. Roasting the tomatoes creates a deep, rich flavor.

1 cup brown basmati rice
1 tbsp. kefir or plain yogurt
12 tomatoes, about 3lb. 5oz., halved
6 garlic cloves, quartered lengthwise
1 large onion, chopped
4 tbsp. olive oil
vegetable bouillon powder for 2 cups water, according to package directions
2 cups vegetable broth

1 Put the rice, kefir, and 2 cups warm water in a medium saucepan and leave to soak, covered, 7 hours, or overnight.

2 Preheat the oven to 400°F. Make a small triangular cut in the stem-end of each tomato half to remove the hard part. Put the tomatoes, cut-side up, in a large baking tray and top each one with 1 slice of garlic. Sprinkle the onion and oil over the tomatoes and bake 1 hour, or until they start to brown.

3 While the tomatoes are baking, bring the rice to a boil over high heat. Stir in the vegetable bouillon powder, then reduce the heat to low and cook, covered, 30 minutes until the rice is just tender.

4 Remove the tomatoes from the oven and transfer them to a large saucepan. Add the vegetable broth and bring to a simmer over medium-high heat, then reduce the heat to low and simmer 30 minutes, stirring occasionally, or until the tomatoes are soft. Blend the mixture with an immersion blender 2 to 3 minutes until completely smooth.

5 Divide the rice into four bowls and pour the soup over. Serve hot.

tomato skins
are an excellent source not only of fiber, but also of flavanoids, a powerful antioxidant, so I never remove them. They puree when you blend the soup, and they help to deepen the flavor of the dish.

creamy rustic soup

This is a great soup for kids because it's substantial enough to be a meal. It's especially good in the fall or winter.

SERVES:
2 adults and
2 children

PREPARATION TIME:
25 minutes,
plus overnight soaking

COOKING TIME:
1 hour 45 minutes

STORAGE:
Refrigerate
up to 3 days
or freeze
up to 3 months.

½ cup pearl barley
⅓ cup spelt
⅓ cup split red lentils
⅓ cup mung beans
1 strip of kombu, about 6 x 2 inches, cut into little pieces
5 tbsp. olive oil
2 onions, chopped
6 garlic cloves, quartered
2 carrots, quartered lengthwise and cut into ¼in.-thick pieces
2 large tomatoes, chopped
3 tbsp. vegetable bouillon powder
hot-pepper sauce, to serve (optional)

1 Put the barley, spelt, red lentils, and mung beans in a large bowl, cover with warm water and leave to soak, covered, overnight.

2 Drain the soaked grain and bean mixture in a strainer and rinse well under cold running water, then transfer to a large saucepan. Add 6 cups water and bring to a boil over high heat. Boil 10 minutes, skimming any scum that rises to the surface, then add the kombu. Reduce the heat to medium-low and simmer, covered, 45 minutes, or until the grains and beans are soft, then discard the kombu.

3 Meanwhile, heat a small saucepan over medium heat. Add 1 tablespoon of the olive oil and when it is hot, add the onions and garlic. Cook 10 minutes, stirring frequently, or until brown, then set aside.

4 When the grain and bean mixture is cooked, add the onions and garlic along with the carrots, tomatoes, and vegetable bouillon. Simmer, covered, over low heat 1 hour longer, stirring occasionally, or until the vegetables are very tender.

5 Divide the soup into four bowls and drizzle each portion with 1 tablespoon of the remaining olive oil. Season the adult portions with the hot-pepper sauce, if using. Serve hot.

barley
adds a richness of flavor plus a good dose of nutrients and fiber to a warming wintry stew. It also provides fuel for the liver and muscles, and will help keep your baby regular.

baked beans with baked potatoes

SERVES:
2 adults and
2 children

PREPARATION
TIME:
35 minutes, plus
overnight soaking

COOKING TIME:
3 hours

STORAGE:
Refrigerate the
beans up to 3 days
or freeze up to
3 months.

Nicholas and Cassie love the slightly sweet, piquant flavor of these baked beans. You'll be surprised how amazing and delicious they are—and how completely different from processed versions. This recipe makes twice as many beans as you need, but serve them over the next few days with eggs or on toast and they'll quickly disappear.

2 cups dried navy
  or great northern
  beans
2 tsp. lemon juice
2 strips of kombu, each
  about 6 x 2 inches, cut
  into tiny pieces
2 onions, chopped
4 garlic cloves, crushed
3 tbsp. olive oil
2 tbsp. molasses
2 tsp. non-hot mustard
3 tbsp. tomato paste
4 Idaho potatoes, pierced
  with a fork
2 tsp. salt

1 Put the beans and lemon juice in a large saucepan, cover with warm water, and leave to soak, covered, overnight.

2 Drain and rinse the beans. Return them to the pan and add 5 cups water. Bring to a boil over high heat and boil 10 minutes, skimming any scum that rises to the surface. Reduce the heat to low, add the kombu, and simmer, covered, 1 hour, or until the beans are soft, then discard the kombu.

3 Preheat the oven to 300°F. Transfer the beans and cooking liquid to a deep, covered Dutch oven. Add the onions, garlic, olive oil, molasses, mustard, and tomato paste and mix well. There should be enough liquid to just cover the beans; if not, add a little extra water. If the beans are cold by the time you are ready to put them in the oven, bring the mixture to a simmer in the Dutch oven over medium-high heat on the stovetop.

4 Put the beans and the potatoes in the oven. Bake, covered, 2 hours, then remove them from the oven. Stir the salt into the beans.

5 Cut open the potatoes, top each one with a few tablespoons of the beans, and serve.

potatoes
have just about
every nutrient, except
vitamin A. For optimum
nutrition, eat them with their
skins on. Cut away and discard
any green parts; these form
when potatoes are exposed
to light, increasing the
levels of solanine,
a toxin.

cherry tomato spaghetti ▶

Broiling makes cherry tomatoes even more delicious—and soft and sloppy to mix with pasta. Children and adults will love this quick meal, which is perfect for when there's a lot of hunger, but not a lot of time.

SERVES:
2 adults and
2 children

PREPARATION TIME:
5 minutes

COOKING TIME:
15 minutes

STORAGE:
Not suitable
for storage.

salt
10oz. dried wholegrain
   spelt spaghetti
9oz. cherry tomatoes
olive oil, to serve

1 Preheat the broiler to medium. Bring a large pan of salted water to a boil and cook the spaghetti according to the package directions.

2 While the spaghetti is cooking, put the tomatoes in a baking dish and broil 5 minutes, or until light brown and beginning to pop. Remove from under the broiler.

3 Drain the spaghetti and divide it into four bowls. Spoon the tomatoes over the top and drizzle with a generous amount of olive oil. Season with salt and serve immediately.

mashed potato craters

A gorgeous way to eat potatoes, this dish is also fun for kids. For variation, you can replace the olive oil with butter or gravy. A hearty mixed salad is a great accompaniment.

SERVES:
2 adults and
2 children

PREPARATION TIME:
15 minutes

COOKING TIME:
20 minutes

STORAGE:
Not suitable
for storage.

2¼lb. Idaho potatoes, cut
   into ¾in. cubes
2 carrots, cut into ½in.
   cubes
3 garlic cloves
½ tsp. salt
4 tbsp. olive oil

1 Put the potatoes, carrots, and garlic in a steamer and steam, covered, over boiling water 20 minutes, or until the potatoes and carrots are soft. Remove from the heat and transfer to a medium bowl, reserving the steam water.

2 Add the salt and a little of the steam water and blend, using an immersion blender, 1 to 2 minutes until smooth and creamy. Add additional steam water, if needed.

3 Using a tablespoon, divide the mixture onto four plates, mounding each portion up into a "mountain." The two adult portions should be twice as big as the two child portions. Using a teaspoon, hollow a crater into the top of each mountain. Pour 4 teaspoons of the olive oil into the adult portions and 2 teaspoons into the child portions. Serve immediately.

wholegrain risotto with asparagus

This nutty, brown-rice risotto has added appeal because of the fresh, lightly steamed asparagus. My kids love the creaminess of this dish and the little bite-size asparagus "logs."

SERVES:
2 adults and
2 children

PREPARATION TIME:
15 minutes, plus at least 7 hours soaking

COOKING TIME:
1 hour 10 minutes

STORAGE:
Not suitable for storage.

1 cup brown arborio rice
1 tsp. kefir or plain yogurt
1½ cups asparagus cut into ¾in. pieces
2 cups vegetable broth
2 tbsp. butter
3 tbsp. olive oil
1 onion, finely chopped

1 Put the rice, kefir and enough warm water to cover in a medium saucepan and soak, covered, for 7 hours, or overnight, then drain.

2 Put the asparagus in a steamer and steam, covered, over boiling water 3 to 5 minutes until just tender, then remove from the heat and set aside. Meanwhile, put the vegetable broth in a medium saucepan. Add 2 cups water and bring to a simmer over medium heat.

3 Heat a large skillet over medium-low heat and add the rice. Heat 10 minutes, stirring frequently, until the rice dries, then transfer it to a dry bowl. Put the butter and oil in the skillet and increase the heat to medium. When the butter melts, add the onion and cook 10 minutes, stirring occasionally with a wooden spoon, until translucent. Add the rice and stir 3 minutes, or until the grains are coated and glossy.

4 Reduce the heat to medium-low. Add 1 ladleful of the stock to the rice and cook 3 to 4 minutes, stirring continuously, until the stock is absorbed. Then add another ladleful of the stock, repeating this process until all of the stock has been added. This will take 35 to 40 minutes. Make sure to keep the risotto at a very gentle simmer, reducing the heat to low, if necessary. When all of the liquid is absorbed, the rice will be creamy and slightly chewy.

5 Stir in the asparagus and cook 3 minutes longer to warm it through. Serve immediately.

asparagus
is a natural diuretic that contributes to healthy gut flora. It's also good for the heart. Besides, asparagus is simply delicious. Your baby will love it paired with other foods or lightly steamed on its own.

chicken & mushroom pasta

Adding raw, grated vegetables to any dish is a great way to increase your child's intake of vitamins and minerals. They also add freshness and flavor.

SERVES:
2 adults and
2 children

PREPARATION
TIME:
15 minutes

COOKING TIME:
25 minutes

STORAGE:
Refrigerate
up to 2 days.

4 tbsp. butter
14oz. boneless, skinless
chicken breast halves
3 cups dried wholegrain
spelt pasta shells
1⅓ cups chopped button
mushrooms
1 small carrot, grated
2 tbsp. olive oil
salt

1 Melt half of the butter in a small skillet over medium-high heat. Season both sides of the chicken with salt and add it to the pan. Cook, covered, 5 minutes on each side, or until cooked through. Transfer the chicken to a plate and leave to cool, then cut it into bite-size pieces.

2 Bring a large saucepan of salted water to a boil and cook the pasta according to the package directions, then drain and transfer to a medium-size serving bowl.

3 Meanwhile, melt the remaining butter in the same skillet over medium-low heat. Add the mushrooms and fry 10 minutes, stirring occasionally, or until light brown.

4 Add the chicken, mushrooms, carrot, and olive oil to the pasta and toss well. Serve warm.

best beef burgers ▶

My dad loved hamburgers when I was growing up—thrown on the barbecue from spring to fall and cooked inside in the winter. The chopped onion transforms ordinary burgers into a wonderful treat.

SERVES:
2 adults and
2 children

PREPARATION
TIME:
10 minutes

COOKING TIME:
10 minutes

STORAGE:
Refrigerate
uncooked burgers
up to 2 days
or freeze up
to 1 month.

1lb. ground beef
1 small onion, finely
chopped
1 tbsp. olive oil
salt and freshly ground
black pepper

To serve (optional):
3 wholegrain spelt
hamburger buns
lettuce
sliced tomato
sliced pickles

1 Put the ground beef and onion in a medium bowl and mix well. Shape some of the mixture into 4 small patties, about 2in. wide and ¾in. high, for child portions. Shape the remaining mixture into 2 patties, about 3½in. wide and ¾in. high, for adult portions. Season each side with salt and pepper and put the patties on a plate.

2 Heat a large skillet over medium-high heat. Add the oil and when it is hot, put the burgers in the pan. Fry, partially covered, 4 to 5 minutes on each side, or until the burgers are crisp and brown. Serve hot. Adults can enjoy this on a wholegrain bun with lettuce, tomato, and pickles, while little mouths will need theirs served with one-quarter to one-half of a bun and the vegetables, if desired.

15 to 24 months

This is the moment the whole family has been waiting for. Once your baby is eating the foods introduced in the chart on page 91, he can eat all family meals. This will simplify your cooking routine tremendously, but you might find yourself shrinking your repertoire of foods back down now that he's eating with you. If you haven't already, make an extra effort to turn the kind of cooking you have been doing for him into a habit, and everyone will be eating well. The recipes in the rest of this chapter will help you do this. It features delicious dishes that will appeal to older children and adults as much as they appeal to your toddler. There's a great mix of options here, using all sorts of ingredients, most of which you're very familiar with by now. Keep trying new things, though, to ensure a good mix of flavors and nutrients in your diet—and you'll find new foods you and your child will love. Remember to continue using salt very sparingly in your cooking, and avoid sugar as much as possible.

CHEESE: You can introduce cheese now, but it's good to offer a variety—not only cow's milk cheeses. Sheep's- and goat's-milk cheeses are best and, of course, organic is heaps better than conventional because there are no antibiotic or pesticide residues to worry about and no growth hormones that can interfere with your child's normal development. Definitely avoid processed cheeses. If you look at the labels on these "cheese products," you'll see that they include all sorts of additives. Don't waste any of your child's —or your own—calories on them.

WHEAT: At this age, you can introduce wheat, but be careful not to rely on it too much. Spelt and Kamut are much better options, and rotating different grains other than those in the wheat family, such as quinoa and millet, is much healthier for all of you. When you buy pasta, don't habitually reach for the wheat versions. The pastas introduced in the first half of this chapter did not include wheat, and there are so many other kinds available. Opt for rice, corn, buckwheat, spelt, and Kamut pastas, and try the different varieties of Japanese noodles available as well. Adding wheat to your child's diet makes it much easier to eat out in restaurants. Most menus feature a pasta dish, which can be great for kids. Restaurants don't usually offer wholewheat pasta, but eating white flour occasionally is fine, so don't worry about allowing your child to eat white pasta when you're out. Just make sure you continue to make whole grains a big part of his diet when you're cooking for him at home.

BREADS: Another great thing about introducing wheat is that you can get more creative with the breads you offer. Give him a variety of different flavors and textures. Try sourdough rye, Irish soda bread, sprouted breads, and spelt bread. (There are two great spelt bread recipes in this book, see pages 142 and 153.) All of these breads taste different and provide your growing toddler with a range of different nutrients.

VEGETABLES: When cooking vegetables now, you can do them *al dente* so they are still firm. This keeps more of the nutrition intact. And remember not to peel vegetables so your child gets all of the fiber and the full range of nutrients. It's good to offer at least two types of vegetables at each meal. I like to serve different colors, with one cooked and one raw. I'm not really into making shapes with food because children naturally like food if it is fresh and well cooked. It can be fun, however, to take a few moments and arrange vegetables into pretty patterns or pictures on the plate.

DRINKS: As mentioned in chapter 3, avoid offering lots of fruit juices. Fruits start to lose nutritional value after juicing, so unless you're juicing at home, most juices don't have much nutrition. It's better to not let children get used to having sweet drinks, anyway. Instead, keep giving your child water to drink. It's a great habit to get into. If he does want a fruity drink, make a smoothie for an afternoon snack. Just throw some chopped fruit into

NEW FOODS TO INTRODUCE AT 15 TO 24 MONTHS

Your child is now ready for the foods listed in the chart below. Combine them with the foods listed in the previous charts to give him the best variety you can.

FRUIT	VEGETABLES	GRAINS	NUTS & SEEDS	DAIRY & EGGS
• grapefruit • orange	• Brussels sprout • samphire • seaweed (all types, including arame, hijiki, kombu and nori)	• wheat	• nuts: almond Brazil nut chestnut hazelnut macadamia nut pecan pine nut pistachio nut walnut	• cheese, especially organic goat's and sheep's milk

your blender along with yogurt, rice milk, or oat milk, and blend until smooth, then serve. Smoothies are naturally sweet, so you never need to add sugar. Or, offer a piece of fruit. He'll get better nutrition from eating an apple than from drinking apple juice.

NUTS & SEEDS: Now that your baby is chewing well, he can start to eat seeds, not just seed oil. He can also have nuts, which are loaded with healthy fats. Chop them up or grind them in a spice mill first, then mix them in with his breakfast cereal or with raisins for a snack. Nut and seed butters are great, too. You can sandwich them between rice cakes or cripsbreads for a convenient snack when you're on the go. Don't rely too heavily on peanut butter, though, and if you are using it, make sure to buy organic. Nonorganic peanuts are one of the most pesticide-laden crops, so you don't want your child exposed to all that chemical residue. Peanuts are also often contaminated with molds that produce aflatoxins, which might be carcinogenic. If there is any family history of nut allergies, wait until age five to introduce them.

ESSENTIAL FATTY-ACID (EFA) SEED MIX: Make a seed mix to have on hand. Put one measure each of sesame seeds and your choice of either sunflower or pumpkin seeds in a jar. Add two measures of flax seeds, seal tightly, and refrigerate away from light, heat, and air. Grind two tablespoons of the mixture in a spice mill at mealtime and mix it into your baby's food. Alternate this with the oils for a nice change and more texture.

CITRUS FRUIT: Oranges and grapefruit are the last fruit I introduce because they are very common allergenic foods. At this age, your child should be able to handle them. Include these fruit in your child's diet occasionally, but make sure to keep giving him lots of other kinds, too. As with other fruit juices, don't let him consume orange juice regularly because he'll want that sweet flavor all the time. It's always better to fill up on food rather than liquids anyway. Once your child is eating these fruit, he can now eat any fruit.

EATING ENOUGH: Again, don't worry if you think he's not eating enough. If he's already feeding himself but you really want to get him to eat more, wait until he's finished, then put some toys on the table. While he's distracted by the toys, you can carry on feeding him some more until he is really full. But one solid meal a day is usually enough between fifteen months and two years. If he's hungry and wants more food, he'll make sure you know it.

Your little one will still need you to cut up most of the dishes that follow. If he isn't chewing enough yet, just wait a little longer and make these recipes when he's older. Also, in the following pages there are recipes for things like hummus, tomato sauce and black bean soup. These delicious recipes are great to make when you have some extra time – they're always good to have around for snacks and quick meals when you don't have that much time to cook.

MEAL PLANNER FOR TODDLERS AT 15 TO 24 MONTHS

Follow this meal planner as closely as you can without stressing out. For variation,
you can alternate seed oils with 2 teaspoons of ground EFA Seed Mix (see page 92).

DAY	BREAKFAST	MID-MORNING	LUNCH	MID-AFTERNOON	DINNER
1	toasted wholewheat pita with tahini	fruit (fresh or dried)	Cheese & Onion Rye Toasts (see page 97) raw carrot steamed broccoli with 2 tsp. seed oil	corn cakes	Roasted Veggies with Feta (see page 95) broiled chicken
2	oatmeal with raisins and yogurt	fruit (fresh or dried)	Lemon–Mackerel, Mayo & Cucumber Sandwiches (see page 104) corn kernels	oatcakes	No-Meat Meatballs (see page 100) with spaghetti and tomato sauce sprouts and lettuce with 2 tsp. seed oil
3	wholegrain rye toast with almond butter	fruit (fresh or dried)	Hummus, Sprouts & Avocado (see page 97) cottage cheese	wholegrain rye crackers/crispbreads	Baked Frittata (see page 99) steamed cauliflower with 2 tsp. seed oil
4	Mustard Scrambled Eggs (see page 78) spelt toast	fruit (fresh or dried)	Arame Rice with Toasted Seeds (see page 105) steamed artichoke hearts with 2 tsp. seed oil	low-salt popcorn	Tuna Pie (see page 107) raw fennel
5	muesli soaked overnight with rice milk	fruit (fresh or dried)	Polenta with Shiitake Mushrooms (see page 98)	Japanese brown rice crackers	Quesadillas (see page 101) Butternut Squash Puree (see page 30) with 2 tsp. EFA Seed Mix (see page 92)
6	puffed rice (no added sugar) with yogurt	fruit (fresh or dried)	Corn & Pea Pancakes (see page 100) sardines	wholewheat grissini or pretzels	Spinach Bake (see page 103) Cucumber & Tomato Salad (see page 151) with 2 tsp. EFA Seed Mix (see page 92)
7	rye toast with mayonnaise and smoked salmon	fruit (fresh or dried)	Kamut Pasta with Veggies & Walnuts (see page 104) Arugula & Lemon Salad (see page 150)	low-salt, baked tortillas	Black Bean Soup with Rice (see page 94) beet with 2 tsp. seed oil

black bean soup with rice

An old family recipe from my mom, this soup has a simplicity that belies its flavor. Kids like it so much that, if you have a large freezer, it's worth making batches of the soup and then freezing it.

SERVES:
4 adults and
4 children

PREPARATION TIME:
20 minutes,
plus overnight
soaking

COOKING TIME:
2 hours 10 minutes

STORAGE:
Refrigerate the
soup up to
3 days or freeze
up to 3 months.
Refrigerate the
rice up to 1 day.
Reheat until hot.

2½ cups dried black turtle beans
2 tsp. lemon juice
2 cups brown basmati rice
1 tbsp. kefir or plain yogurt
1 strip of kombu, about 6 x 2in., cut into little pieces
1 large onion, finely chopped
⅔ cup olive oil
5 tbsp. white wine vinegar
5 garlic cloves, crushed
1 yellow bell pepper, seeded and chopped
½ tsp. dried oregano
1 tbsp. ground cumin
4 tsp. salt
hot-pepper sauce, to serve (optional)

1 Put the beans and lemon juice in a large saucepan, cover with warm water, and leave to soak, covered, overnight.

2 Put the rice, kefir, and 4⅓ cups warm water in a medium saucepan and leave to soak, covered, for 7 hours or overnight.

3 Drain and rinse the beans. Return them to the pan and add 8¾ cups water. Bring to a boil over high heat and boil 10 minutes, skimming any scum that rises to the surface. Reduce the heat to low, add the kombu, and simmer, covered, 1 hour, or until the beans are soft.

4 When the beans have cooked halfway, bring the rice to a boil over high heat, then reduce the heat to low and cook, covered, 30 minutes, or until just tender. As soon as the rice has finished cooking, remove it from the heat and stir in half of the onion, 3 tablespoons of the olive oil, and 2 teaspoons of the vinegar. Set aside and leave to marinate 1 hour, or until the soup is ready.

5 Add the garlic, yellow bell pepper, oregano, cumin, and the remaining onion to the beans. Stir in the remaining 4 tablespoons vinegar and continue cooking, covered, 1 hour longer, stirring occasionally, or until the beans are very soft. Stir in the salt and the remaining ½ cup of the olive oil.

6 Put some of the rice in four bowls and top with 1 ladleful of the soup. Season the adult portions with the hot-pepper sauce, if using. Serve hot.

slow cooking
fresh, wholesome
ingredients at a low
temperature for a long time
creates a delicious, nutritious
meal with meltingly tender
components—and as with this
soup, the goodness from the
vegetables and legumes
stays in the pot.

roasted veggies with feta ▼

SERVES:
2 adults and
2 children

PREPARATION
TIME:
20 minutes

COOKING TIME:
25 minutes

STORAGE:
Refrigerate
up to 3 days.

The roasted garlic combined with rosemary and oven-browned feta cheese in this dish makes a fabulous mix. Children love the different-colored vegetables, which are sweet and delicious when roasted.

4 tbsp. olive oil
2 potatoes, cut into small
cubes
1 carrot, quartered
lengthwise and sliced
into rounds
10 garlic cloves
½ tsp. dried rosemary
½ cup bite-size broccoli
florets
1 small red bell pepper,
seeded and cut into
small pieces
6oz. feta cheese, cut into
small cubes

1 Preheat the oven to 500°F and grease a medium roasting pan or baking dish with 1 tablespoon of the olive oil. Put the potatoes, carrot, garlic, rosemary, and 2 tablespoons of the remaining olive oil in a large bowl and mix well, then pour them into the baking dish. Bake 15 minutes, or until the vegetables begin to soften.

2 Meanwhile, put the broccoli, red bell pepper, feta cheese, and remaining 1 tablespoon of olive oil in another bowl and mix well.

3 Remove the vegetables from the oven and stir in the broccoli mixture. Bake 10 minutes longer, or until the vegetables and feta are beginning to brown. Serve hot.

◀ hummus, sprouts & avocado

SERVES:
2 adults and
2 children

PREPARATION TIME:
20 minutes, plus overnight soaking

COOKING TIME:
2 hours 10 minutes

STORAGE:
Refrigerate the hummus up to 3 days.

This is a delicious reminder of why hummus is great to have in the fridge – and when you make your own, you control how much salt goes into it.

½ cup dried chickpeas
3 tbsp. plus 2 tsp. lemon juice
1 strip of kombu, about 3¼ x 2 inches
2 garlic cloves, crushed
1 tbsp. tahini
4 tbsp. olive oil
¼ tsp. salt
6 slices of wholegrain spelt bread
2 avocados, halved, pitted, peeled, and sliced
2oz. alfalfa sprouts
½ lemon, cut into 4 wedges

1 Put the chickpeas and 2 teaspoons of the lemon juice in a medium saucepan, cover with warm water, and leave to soak, covered, overnight.

2 Drain and rinse the chickpeas and return them to the pan. Add 3 cups water and bring to a boil over high heat. Boil 10 minutes, skimming any scum that rises to the surface, then reduce the heat to low, add the kombu and cook, covered, 2 hours, or until soft. Remove from the heat and leave the chickpeas to cool completely in the cooking water.

3 Drain and rinse well, then put the chickpeas and kombu in a blender. Add the garlic, tahini, olive oil, salt, remaining lemon juice, and 4 tablespoons water. Blend 1 to 2 minutes until smooth.

4 Toast the bread and then spread 1 tablespoon of the hummus on each slice and top with a few slices of the avocado. Divide the sprouts over the avocado, then squeeze the lemon wedges over. Cut into strips and serve immediately.

cheese & onion rye toasts

SERVES:
2 adults and
2 children

PREPARATION TIME:
10 minutes

COOKING TIME:
4 minutes

STORAGE:
Not suitable for storage.

This is a cross between an American grilled cheese sandwich and English cheese on toast. The red onion softens while the cheese melts underneath, creating a flavor and texture your little ones will find delightful.

6 slices of wholegrain rye bread
non-hot mustard, to taste, for spreading
6oz. sharp cheddar cheese, cut into ¼in.-thick slices
1 red onion, sliced into rings and quartered

1 Preheat the broiler to medium. Meanwhile, toast the bread in a toaster, then spread a little mustard on one side of each slice and put them on a large cookie sheet. Divide the cheese over the toasts, covering well, then evenly arrange the onion over the cheese.

2 Broil 4 minutes, or until the onion is soft and the cheese is beginning to melt. Serve hot.

polenta with shiitake mushrooms

Polenta is wonderfully versatile, and children love its subtle, sweet flavor. When you feel like experimenting, try mixing in extra ingredients, such as six whole garlic cloves, a chopped onion, and/or grated cheese, in step 1.

SERVES:
2 adults and
2 children

PREPARATION TIME:
15 minutes

COOKING TIME:
45 minutes

STORAGE:
Refrigerate the polenta and mushrooms separately up to 3 days.

2 tbsp. butter, plus extra for greasing
1 cup cornmeal
1 tsp. salt
1 onion, finely chopped
1 garlic clove, finely chopped
1 tsp. dried thyme
1lb. shiitake mushrooms, brushed clean, stems discarded, and caps sliced
¾ cup Greek-style plain yogurt

1 Grease a 12-inch round baking dish with butter and set aside. Put 3¾ cups water in a heavy-bottomed saucepan and bring to a boil over high heat. Reduce the heat to medium and pour in the cornmeal, whisking continuously with a metal whisk until smooth. Stir in the salt and then reduce the heat to low. Cook 15 minutes, stirring continuously with a wooden spoon, or until the polenta is thick and rubbery, then pour it into the baking dish and smooth the top using a rubber spatula. Leave to cool and set.

2 While the polenta is cooling, make the mushroom mixture. Melt the butter in a large skillet over medium-high heat. Add the onion and cook 5 minutes, stirring, until light brown. Add the garlic and thyme and continue cooking 3 minutes longer, stirring occasionally.

3 Increase the heat to high and add the mushrooms. Cook 10 minutes, stirring continuously, or until the mushrooms are golden brown. Remove from the heat and stir in the yogurt, then set aside.

4 Preheat the broiler to medium. Cut the polenta into 8 wedges and broil in the baking dish 5 minutes, or until warm and crisp.

5 Divide the broiled polenta onto plates and spoon 2 tablespoons of the mushroom mixture over the tops. Serve immediately.

shiitake mushrooms
are potently flavorful and have been used medicinally by the Chinese for more than 6,000 years. They contain an active compound called lentinan, which strengthens the immune system so it can fight infection and disease.

▼ baked frittata

A frittata is a type of Italian omelet that can include meats, cheeses, and vegetables. It is usually cooked on the stovetop and then broiled to finish.

SERVES:
2 adults and
2 children

**PREPARATION
TIME:**
15 minutes

COOKING TIME:
55 minutes

STORAGE:
Refrigerate
up to 3 days.

butter, for greasing
**2 cups unpeeled red
   potatoes chopped into
   ⅝in. cubes**
2 tsp. olive oil
1 onion, chopped
5 eggs, beaten
**½ bag (10oz.) frozen
   spinach, chopped**
**1½ cups feta cheese
   cut into ½in. cubes**
**½ cup pitted, sliced
   Kalamata olives**
**hot-pepper sauce
   (optional), to serve**

1 Preheat the oven to 400°F and generously grease a large pie plate or round baking dish with butter. Bring a large saucepan of water to a boil and cook the potatoes 10 minutes, or until soft. Remove from the heat, drain, and leave to cool.

2 Heat the oil in a medium skillet over medium heat. When the oil is hot, add the onion and cook 10 minutes, stirring occasionally, or until brown. Stir in the potatoes, eggs, spinach, feta, and olives and mix well, then pour the mixture into the baking dish. Bake 25 to 30 minutes until the egg is just cooked.

3 Meanwhile, preheat the broiler to medium. Transfer the baking dish to the top shelf under the broiler and broil 3 minutes, or until the cheese is light brown. Serve hot with the hot-pepper sauce, if using.

no-meat meatballs

Lovely and cheesy with a hint of onion and oregano, these succulent tofu balls are a delicious alternative to more conventional meatballs.

SERVES:
2 adults and 2 children

PREPARATION TIME:
30 minutes, plus making the tomato sauce

COOKING TIME:
35 minutes

STORAGE:
Refrigerate up to 2 days.

2 tsp. olive oil, plus extra for greasing
1 small onion, chopped
2 slices of wholewheat or wholegrain spelt bread, lightly toasted
14oz. firm tofu, drained
3 eggs, beaten
3 tbsp. grated cheddar cheese
¼ tsp. salt, plus extra for cooking the pasta
1 tsp. dried oregano
10oz. dried spelt pasta
½ recipe quantity Tomato Sauce (see page 117)

1 Preheat the oven to 350°F and grease a large baking dish with olive oil. Heat the olive oil in a small skillet over medium-high heat, add the onion, and cook 5 minutes, stirring occasionally, or until it begins to soften. Meanwhile, lightly toast the bread, then put it in a blender and blend for 1 minute until bread crumbs form.

2 Crumble the tofu into a large bowl. Add the bread crumbs, onion, eggs, cheddar, salt, and oregano and mix well with a fork.

3 Shape the mixture into 20 equal-size balls and put them in the baking dish. Bake 30 minutes. Meanwhile, bring a large pan of salted water to a boil and cook the pasta according to the package directions, then drain and transfer to a serving bowl. Heat the tomato sauce and serve hot with the pasta and no-meat meatballs.

corn & pea pancakes

These simple, savory pancakes are a great way to get your child to eat his peas. They're good on their own, but for variation try them served with yogurt on the side or with grated cheese sprinkled on top.

SERVES:
2 adults and 2 children

PREPARATION TIME:
10 minutes

COOKING TIME:
20 minutes

STORAGE:
Refrigerate the cooked pancakes up to 3 days.

1 cup wholegrain spelt flour
1 tsp. baking powder
2 eggs, beaten
⅔ cup milk
¾ cup shelled peas
¾ cup corn kernels
½ tsp. salt
1 tsp. olive oil

1 Preheat the oven to 150°F. Put the flour and baking powder in a medium bowl and mix well. Whisk in the eggs and milk until smooth and then stir in the peas, corn, and salt.

2 Heat the olive oil in a large skillet over medium-low heat until hot. Pour tablespoonfuls of the batter into the pan, spacing well apart, and cook 2 to 3 minutes on each side until light brown. Alternatively, cook the pancakes on a griddle over medium-low heat 2 to 3 minutes on each side until light brown. Transfer to a plate and keep warm in the oven while you make the remaining pancakes. Serve hot.

quesadillas

Quesadillas are so quick to make—and I haven't yet met a child who doesn't like them. You can lift the flavor by sprinkling a few sliced scallions over the cheese.

SERVES:
2 adults and
2 children

PREPARATION TIME:
10 minutes, plus overnight soaking

COOKING TIME:
1 hour 40 minutes

STORAGE:
Refrigerate the beans up to 3 days.

½ cup dried adzuki beans
2 tsp. lemon juice
1 strip of kombu, about
   3¼ x 2 inches, cut into
   little pieces
½ tsp. salt
1¾ cups grated cheddar
   cheese
12 flour tortillas

1 Put the beans and lemon juice in a medium saucepan, cover with warm water, and leave to soak, covered, overnight.

2 Drain and rinse the beans. Return them to the pan and add 3 cups water. Bring to a boil over high heat and boil 10 minutes, skimming any scum that rises to the surface. Reduce the heat to low, add the kombu and cook, covered, 1 hour, or until the beans are soft. Check occasionally to ensure the beans remain covered with water and add extra boiling water, if necessary. Drain well, then return to the pan and stir in the salt.

3 Preheat the oven to 150°F. Heat a large skillet over medium heat until hot. Put 1 tortilla in the pan, sprinkle with 1 tablespoon of the cheddar, followed by a few tablespoons of the beans and then another tablespoon of the cheddar. Cover with a second tortilla and cook 3 to 4 minutes until the underside of the bottom tortilla is light brown and the cheese melts.

4 Slide a spatula under the tortilla and put your fingertips on top of the top tortilla, then flip it over and cook the other side 3 minutes, or until light brown. Slide the quesadilla onto a plate and keep warm in the oven while you make the remaining quesadillas. When ready to serve, cut the quesadillas into wedges, using a sharp knife or pizza cutter, and serve warm.

adzuki beans
are one of the highest-protein and lowest-fat varieties of bean. They're also rich in soluble fiber, which helps digestion. Traditional Chinese medicine claims adzuki beans benefit the bladder and kidneys, too.

spinach bake

This is a recipe I have really perfected over the years. We love the browned cheese and the toasty pine nuts.

SERVES:
2 adults and
2 children

PREPARATION TIME:
20 minutes, plus at least 7 hours soaking

COOKING TIME:
1 hour 20 minutes

STORAGE:
Refrigerate up to 3 days. Reheat until hot.

1 cup brown basmati rice
1 tbsp. kefir or plain yogurt
2 cups vegetable broth
⅓ cup pine nuts
butter, for greasing
1 tbsp. olive oil
1 large onion, finely chopped
4 eggs
8oz. frozen chopped spinach, thawed
1¾ cups grated cheddar cheese
1 tbsp. gluten-free vegetarian Worcestershire sauce
1 tsp. dried thyme
1 tsp. dried rosemary

1 Put the rice, kefir, and 2 cups warm water in a medium saucepan and leave to soak, covered, 7 hours, or overnight.

2 Drain the rice, then return it to the pan and add the vegetable broth. Bring to a boil over high heat and stir, then cover and reduce the heat to low. Simmer 30 minutes, or until the rice is cooked.

3 Meanwhile, preheat the broiler to medium. Put the pine nuts on a cookie sheet and broil 2 to 3 minutes until light brown, checking frequently to ensure they don't burn. Set aside.

4 Preheat the oven to 400°F and grease an 8- x 8-inch baking dish with butter. Heat the oil in a skillet, add the onion, and cook over medium heat 3 to 4 minutes, stirring occasionally, until translucent. Remove from the heat.

5 Put the eggs and spinach in a blender and blend 1 to 2 minutes until smooth, then transfer to a large bowl.

6 Add the pine nuts, onion, cheddar, Worcestershire sauce, thyme, and rosemary to the spinach mixture and mix well. Stir in the rice, then spoon the mixture into the baking dish.

7 Bake 45 minutes, or until light brown. Leave to cool 5 minutes, then serve.

spinach
is a nutritional star. It's rich in antioxidants, which support your child's immune system, and it's loaded with vitamins and minerals, including vitamins A and C and magnesium.

kamut pasta with veggies & walnuts

Toasting the walnuts makes all the difference in flavor in this delicious pasta dish my children love.

SERVES:
2 adults and
2 children

PREPARATION
TIME:
30 minutes

COOKING TIME:
25 minutes

STORAGE:
Not suitable
for storage.

½ tsp. salt, plus extra for cooking the pasta
2 cups broccoli florets
1 cup walnut halves, chopped
3 cups dried Kamut pasta
½ cup plus 2 tsp. olive oil
1 onion, chopped
3 garlic cloves, chopped
10 basil leaves, torn
½ tsp. salt

1 Preheat the broiler to medium and bring a large pan of salted water to a boil. Put the broccoli in a steamer and steam, covered, over boiling water 5 minutes, or until just soft. Meanwhile, put the walnuts on a small baking tray and broil 4 to 5 minutes until just beginning to brown. Remove from the heat and leave to cool.

2 Cook the pasta according to the package directions. Meanwhile, heat a medium skillet over medium heat and add 2 teaspoons of the olive oil. When the oil is hot, add the onion and cook, stirring, 8 minutes, or until light brown. Add the garlic and continue cooking 2 minutes longer.

3 When the pasta has finished cooking, drain it and transfer to a large bowl. Add the onion mixture, broccoli, walnuts, basil, salt, and remaining olive oil and mix well. Serve warm.

lemon–mackerel, mayo & cucumber sandwiches

This is great for lunch—or lunchboxes when your child is older. The lemon juice adds freshness to the oily fish and the cucumber adds crunch.

SERVES:
1 adult and 1 child

PREPARATION
TIME:
10 minutes

STORAGE:
Refrigerate the
mackerel mixture
up to 3 days.

4¼oz. smoked mackerel
2 tbsp. mayonnaise, plus extra for spreading
3 tsp. lemon juice
4 slices of wholewheat bread
8 cucumber slices

1 Remove and discard the skin from the mackerel and remove any bones, feeling the flesh with your fingers. Shred the mackerel into a small bowl with a fork. Add the mayonnaise and lemon juice and mix well.

2 Spread each slice of bread with a little mayonnaise. Put the cucumber slices on two slices of the bread and spread the mackerel on top of them. Cover with the remaining slices of bread, cut each sandwich diagonally into two triangles, and serve.

arame rice with toasted seeds

Seaweed is the perfect way to add not only extra flavor, but extra goodness, too. Toasted seeds make any dish more interesting because their roasted flavor is so good.

SERVES:
2 adults and
2 children

PREPARATION TIME:
10 minutes,
plus overnight
soaking

COOKING TIME:
30 minutes

STORAGE:
Refrigerate
up to 1 day.
Reheat until hot.

1 cup brown basmati rice
1 tbsp. kefir or plain
    yogurt
⅛oz. arame
2 tbsp. sunflower seeds,
    pulsed in a blender
2 tbsp. pumpkin seeds,
    pulsed in a blender
1 tsp. tamari soy sauce
4 tbsp. olive oil

1 Put the rice, kefir, and 2 cups warm water in a medium saucepan and leave to soak, covered, 7 hours, or overnight.

2 Bring the rice to a boil over high heat, then reduce the heat to low and cook, covered, 30 minutes, or until the rice is just tender.

3 Meanwhile, crumble the arame into a bowl, using your hands or a mortar and pestle, and cover with boiled water. Leave to soak 15 minutes, then drain.

4 While the rice is cooking, heat a medium skillet over medium heat. When it is hot, add the sunflower and pumpkin seeds and the tamari and cook 3 to 4 minutes, stirring with a wooden spoon, until lightly toasted and dry.

5 Transfer the seeds to a medium serving bowl and add the rice, arame, and olive oil. Mix well and serve warm or at room temperature.

seaweeds
are low in calories and
rich in essential minerals,
vitamins, and protein. They
are also rich in very important
trace elements that are often
missing from conventional
land vegetables because of
the depletion of minerals
from the soil.

tuna pie

The pie is so simple, and the combination of flavors is perfect. Wholegrain pastry is a must—the one used here is nutritious and easy to handle. Make sure to always buy sustainably sourced tuna (see page 40).

SERVES:
2 adults and
2 children

PREPARATION TIME:
50 minutes, plus
30 minutes chilling

COOKING TIME:
45 minutes

STORAGE:
Refrigerate the dough up to 3 days or freeze up to 3 months. If you are not going to use the dough the day you make it, mix in 1 tablespoon plain yogurt when you add the cold water. The baked pie is best eaten straightaway.

1 cup wholegrain spelt flour, plus extra for rolling
¾ tsp. salt
6 tbsp. butter, cut into pieces
4 tbsp. tomato paste
3¼oz. canned tuna in water or oil, drained
1 large tomato, sliced
1 tsp. dried basil
1 tsp. dried oregano
4oz. buffalo mozzarella cheese, drained and sliced
1 cup pitted Kalamata olives, sliced

tuna
is an excellent source of omega-3 essential fatty acids, protein, and many important minerals. Both fresh and canned tuna are delicious, but many varieties of tuna are severely overfished, so make always read labels and buy sustainably sourced tuna.

1 Put the flour and ½ teaspoon of the salt in a medium bowl and mix well. Using a pastry cutter, cut in the butter until the particles are the size of small peas. If you don't have a pastry cutter, rub the butter into the flour using two knives or your fingertips. Add 3 tablespoons cold water and toss the mixture with a fork until the dough is moist enough to hold together. Shape into a short log, wrap in plastic wrap, and refrigerate 30 minutes.

2 Preheat the oven to 400°F. Cut off about one-third of the dough from the log, rewrap, and set aside. Lightly sprinkle a large piece of baking parchment with flour and, using a rolling pin, roll out the larger piece of dough to about 12 inches in diameter. Hold a 9in. pie plate over the dough to estimate the size. Lift the parchment paper and turn it over to drop the dough into the pie plate, then press the dough in to fit and press out any air pockets. Lightly sprinkle a new piece of baking parchment with flour and roll the remaining pastry into a 12-inch-wide circle and set aside.

3 Spread the tomato paste over the bottom of the dough to coat. Cover with half the tuna, followed by half the tomato slices, half the basil and oregano, half the mozzarella, and half the olives. Sprinkle with half the remaining salt, then continue layering, starting with the remaining tomato slices, basil, oregano, mozzarella, olives, and salt and ending with the remaining tuna.

4 Cover the top of the pie with the remaining dough. Fold the edges of the bottom crust over the edges of the top crust and press together with your fingers to flute. Carefully cut a "T" into the middle of the top crust with a sharp knife to allow air to circulate during baking.

5 Bake 45 minutes, or until the crust is light brown and the pie is bubbling in the middle. Cut and serve hot.

forks & knives

Now that your child is feeding herself and eating with the rest of the family, you can cook foods that are more sophisticated and require more coordination to eat. She'll have fun assembling Make-Your-Own Sushi and digging into the grown-up flavors found in dishes such as Shrimp Pasta Bake and Curried Rice with Cranberries & Almonds. Let her help with easy tasks in the kitchen, too. This can be great fun and can spark a deeper interest in food. She might be little, but there's usually something to be poured, added or stirred that even little hands can manage—and when a child helps make something, she usually really wants to eat it when it's ready. She can also just sit and watch while you explain what you're doing. It's a great way to spend time together and for her to learn.

Blueberry Loaf (see page 135)

2 to 3 years

Your child's digestive tract is now mature, so she can eat anything you can. Remember, though, it's normal for a child's appetite to change. She'll be hungrier as she heads toward growth spurts, less so when she is tired or getting sick. Don't worry if she doesn't seem to be eating as much as you think she should. Always serve meals and encourage her to eat and then ensure she's getting healthy snacks as well. Some children are more into grazing, especially when they are little. If you write down what she actually eats during a day, you'll probably be surprised at how much it is.

DEALING WITH A FUSSY CHILD: Whereas your baby was compliant and would try anything, your toddler might like to argue with you about all sorts of things now and might not be so willing to try new foods. A great gift you can give her is to try foods with an open mind. If she says, "I don't like that," when she sees something new, explain that it might become her most favorite food in the entire world, but she won't know unless she tries it. Make it a game. Ask her to try something with her eyes closed. Can she guess what it is? If you can, take her food shopping and let her choose something new to try a few times a month. If she chooses something you've never had before, then you can learn together how to cook and eat it. There should be no pressure to eat something new, only encouragement or excitement—or reverse psychology: "You don't want to try that!" or "That's so yummy, I'm saving it for me and Daddy." Whatever works with your child. Don't assume she won't like something just because she is little, either. She might just surprise you. From when they were very young, my kids loved roasted artichoke hearts, broiled garlic, and caper berries.

If she starts to get fussy about eating vegetables, there are some great ways to encourage and get her engaged with her food. Try offering a bowl of vegetables cut into bite-size pieces with olives, peas, or corn kernels to be eaten with a toothpick. Or, mix the vegetables with mayonnaise, tzatziki, yogurt, or a little olive oil and balsamic vinegar and a light sprinkle of salt. You can also offer a bowl of vegetables with a bowl of oil, tahini, hummus, mayonnaise, tzatziki, or yogurt for dipping. When she is starving and can't possibly wait while you cook supper, put the veggies on the table first.

HELPING IN THE KITCHEN: Getting your child involved in the kitchen is another way to encourage her interest in food. Make the Baked Artichoke Hearts and let her cut the soft artichokes in half with a blunt knife. Teach her how to beat an egg for the Potato & Parsnip Pancakes. Let her arrange the almonds for the Curried Rice on the baking tray and then taste how different they are raw versus after they're roasted and have cooled

WONDERFOODS TO INCLUDE REGULARLY IN YOUR CHILD'S MEALS

The foods listed here are nutritional powerhouses. Include them in your child's diet as often as you can.

FOOD	MAIN NUTRIENTS	BENEFITS TO CHILDREN	INTRODUCE THIS FOOD AT ...	RECIPES CONTAINING THIS FOOD
apples	Vitamin C, pectin, malic, and tartaric acid	Detoxifier	4 to 6 months	Apple Puree (see page 26) Rice & Mango Breakfast (see page 42)
almonds	Vitamin E, potassium, and magnesium; high in monounsaturated fat	Aids absorption of calcium	15 to 24 months	Curried Rice with Cranberries & Almonds (see page 121)
avocado	Oleic acid, potassium, folate, lutein, vitamin E	Anticancer	4 to 6 months	Avocado Mash (see page 28) Guacamole (see page 144)
broccoli	Indols, carotenoids, iron	Anticancer	4 to 6 months	Saucy Steam-Fry (see page 62) Roasted Veggies with Feta (see page 95)
oily fish	Omega-3 fats, EPA, and protein	Builds brain and nerve tissue	6 to 9 months	Salmon & Peas (see page 48) Tuna Pie (see page 107)
pumpkin and squash	Antioxidants, including beta-carotene and the rest of the carotenoids	Protect against infection	4 to 6 months	Fava Bean & Pumpkin Puree (see page 45) Squash & Potato Soup (see page 80)
seeds	Omega-6 fats and omega-3 fats, zinc, magnesium, and calcium	Anticancer; reduces risk of allergies and eczema	oil, from 4 to 6 months; ground or chopped, from 15 to 24 months	Muesli Cookies (see page 133) Sesame & Raisin Bread Balls (see page 153)
seaweeds	Vitamin K, iodine, chlorophyll, and alginic acid	Aids good thyroid function; detoxifier	4 to 6 months, for cooking beans; 15 to 24 months, for direct feeding	Arame Rice with Toasted Seeds (see page 105) Make-Your-Own Sushi (see page 122)
sprouted beans and sprouted seeds	Enzymes	Improves digestion	9 to 12 months	Brown Rice & Sprouts (see page 65) Toasted Quinoa & Vegetable Salad (see page 126)
whole grains	Fiber, B vitamins, iron, magnesium, and selenium	Aids regular bowel function	4 to 6 months	Cornbread Pudding (see page 79) Chicken with Apricot & Fennel Wild Rice (see page 130)
live, plain yogurt	Healthy bacteria; protein; calcium; phosphorus; vitamins B2, B12, B5; zinc	Strengthens immune system	4 to 6 months, for soaking grains; 9 to 12 months, for direct feeding	Snow Peas, Cucumber & Yogurt Salad (see page 67) Shrimp Pasta Bake (see page 129)

down. For other dishes, she can pour ingredients in or mix them. She'll love being with you—and she'll love helping.

OPTIMIZING NUTRITION: The chart on page 111 will help you to remember the wonderfoods that should form a regular part of your child's diet, if they don't already. We're all so busy that it's easy to fall back on old habits or cook the same thing again and again. We all do it. This list and the charts in this book will help to steer you back on track when you get in a rut. Sometimes life is so hectic that everything gets simplified. When that happens, you might find it hard to think, so just glance at the chart and remember it doesn't take much time to sprinkle hemp seeds on cereal, mix vegetables with yogurt, or add chopped sprouts to a pasta dish. When things ease up and you have a little more time again, make the dishes that require a bit more time.

AVOIDING SWEETS: Above all, don't be tempted to give your child junk food or candy "just so she eats something." It's actually better that she doesn't eat because then she'll eat whatever you give her when she is hungry. It's just not worth creating bad habits. If she hasn't eaten lunch and then asks for a chocolate bar in the afternoon, don't give in. If you do, she'll ask for it all the time. Sometimes you can avoid the argument or distract her by ignoring her request and cutting up an apple or other fruit she likes and putting in on the table without saying anything. I like to have a bowl of fruit, nuts, and healthy snacks, such as wholewheat pretzels, wholegrain crispbreads, or brown rice crackers, on the table or the counter where children can see it. This way, they can help themselves.

I don't offer a lot of desserts. I certainly don't have desserts after every meal or every day. There's no reason to have something sweet twice a day. It sets up a habit that can be very difficult to reverse. When there is no dessert at the end of a meal, kids are less likely to refuse to eat just because they know a more appealing dessert is coming.

BROWN RICE SYRUP: When I do bake, I always try to reduce the amount of sugar. With some baked goods, like banana bread, you can almost do without sugar entirely. It's also better to use brown rice syrup than granulated sugar or even maple syrup, which are simple carbohydrates and cause a rush of energy followed by the sugar blues. Brown rice syrup contains about 30 percent soluble complex carbohydrates, 45 percent maltose (grain-malt sugar), and only 3 to 4 percent glucose (and 20 percent water). Although the glucose hits the bloodstream almost immediately, the maltose takes up to 1½ hours to digest, while the complex carbs are digested and released for up to 4 hours, so the overall effect on blood sugar levels is much gentler than with simple sugars. If you want to convert old recipes you have or new recipes you would like to try, for every 1 cup sugar, use ¾ cup brown rice syrup and reduce liquids by ¼ cup.

There are a few recipes for sweet baked goods in this chapter. They're nice to have occasionally in the afternoons or on the weekends when everyone likes something special.

MEAL PLANNER FOR CHILDREN AT 2 TO 3 YEARS

Here's an idea of how to work the recipes in this chapter into your child's diet.
Just do your best, cook in batches when you can and always add nutrition.

DAY	BREAKFAST	MID-MORNING	LUNCH	MID-AFTERNOON	DINNER
1	wholegrain rye toast with almond butter and yogurt	fruit (fresh or dried)	Shrimp Pasta Bake (see page 129) steamed broccoli with 2 tsp. seed oil raw carrot	Blueberry Loaf (see page 135)	Pecan & Stilton Stuffed Mushrooms (see page 118) arugula and sprouts salad
2	overnight oatmeal with soaked dried fruit	fruit (fresh or dried)	Hot Sardine Toasts (see page 128) steamed cauliflower raw peas	oatcakes with tahini	Chicken with Apricot & Fennel Wild Rice (see page 130) with 2 tsp. seed oil avocado
3	Potato & Parsnip Pancakes (see page 116)	fruit (fresh or dried)	Baked Mushroom Open Sandwich with Tomato Sauce (see page 117) apple slices	Date, Oat & Hazelnut Bars (see page 134)	Haddock with Capers (see page 128) celery sticks steamed carrots with 2 tsp. seed oil
4	Fruit Ambrosia (see page 60) sprouted bread	fruit (fresh or dried)	Potato & Egg Salad (see page 125) cucumber sticks nori squares	hummus (see page 97) with 2 tsp. seed oil wholewheat grissini	Pork with Gherkins (see page 131) snow peas mashed sweet potato (see Carrot Puree on page 79)
5	scrambled eggs with Irish soda bread toast	fruit (fresh or dried)	Noodles with Vegetables (see page 125)	mixed nuts and seeds	Chili non Carne (see page 114) with grated cheese and tortillas spinach leaf salad and hemp seeds
6	Cornbread Pudding (see page 79) cottage cheese	fruit (fresh or dried)	Toasted Quinoa & Vegetable Salad (see page 126) sardines	Muesli Cookies (see page 133)	Make-Your-Own Sushi (see page 122) Baked Artichoke Hearts (see page 115)
7	Spelt French Toast (see page 79)	fruit (fresh or dried)	Curried Rice with Cranberries & Almonds (see page 121) broiled parsnip	rye crackers with goat cheese	Brussels Sprouts & Barley Stew (see page 116) beet and yogurt salad with 2 tsp. seed oil

chili non carne

My husband Brian's favorite, this hearty chili features weekly on my meal planner. If your children don't like spicy foods, reduce the cayenne pepper to ¼ teaspoon. If you want to make a meat chili, use beef instead of the tempeh. Brown six ounces ground beef in 2 tablespoons olive oil and add it to the chili mixture 20 minutes before the dish finishes cooking.

SERVES:
2 adults and
2 children

PREPARATION TIME:
25 minutes, plus overnight soaking

COOKING TIME:
2 hours 40 minutes

STORAGE:
Refrigerate the vegetarian chilli up to 3 days and the beef chilli up to 2 days.

¾ cup dried pinto beans
2 tsp. lemon juice
1 strip of kombu, about 6 x 2 inches
1 tbsp. olive oil
1 large onion, chopped
2 garlic cloves, crushed
6oz. tempeh, cut into small cubes
1 orange bell pepper, seeded and chopped
3⅓ cups chopped canned tomatoes
½ tsp. cayenne pepper
¾ tsp. salt
1½ cups grated sharp cheddar cheese
7oz. low-salt corn chips (optional)

1 Put the beans and lemon juice in a medium saucepan, cover with warm water, and leave to soak, covered, overnight.

2 Drain and rinse the beans. Return them to the pan and add 2½ cups water. Bring to a boil over high heat and boil 10 minutes, skimming any scum that rises to the surface. Reduce the heat to low, add the kombu and cook, covered, 2 hours, or until soft.

3 Meanwhile, heat a large saucepan over medium-low heat and add the olive oil. When the oil is hot, add the onion and cook 8 minutes, stirring continuously, until light brown. Add the garlic and cook, stirring, 2 minutes longer. Stir in the tempeh, orange bell pepper, tomatoes, and cayenne pepper.

4 Mash together the beans, kombu, and cooking liquid and add to the tempeh mixture. Cook, covered, 1 hour, stirring occasionally, or until well cooked and the flavors come together.

5 Stir in the salt and sprinkle the chili generously with the cheddar. Serve by itself or with the corn chips, if desired.

tempeh is a naturally fermented soy food. It contains vitamin B12, which is vital for brain and nerve health, as well as probiotic bacteria, which support good digestive health.

▼ baked artichoke hearts

SERVES:
2 adults and
2 children

We love artichokes any which way, but combining them with crunchy, roasted garlic and zingy lemon zest makes this beautiful dish divine. Jessica can eat almost half of this dish all by herself!

PREPARATION
TIME:
15 minutes

COOKING TIME:
30 minutes

STORAGE:
Refrigerate
up to 3 days.

3 tbsp. olive oil, plus extra for greasing
1 slice of wholewheat bread or ½ cup bread crumbs
½ cup grated Parmesan cheese
4 garlic cloves, finely chopped
1 tbsp. chopped parsley
2lb. 2oz. canned artichoke hearts in water, drained, squeezed, and halved lengthwise
juice and zest of ½ lemon

1 Preheat the oven to 350° and grease a 9-inch round baking dish with olive oil. If using fresh bread, lightly toast it and then put it in a blender. Blend 1 minute, or until bread crumbs form. Put the bread crumbs in a small bowl and mix in the olive oil, Parmesan, garlic, parsley, and lemon juice and zest.

2 Top each artichoke half with 1 teaspoon of the bread-crumb mixture and put the artichokes mixture-side up in the baking dish.

3 Sprinkle any remaining bread-crumb mixture in the baking dish and bake 30 minutes, or until golden brown. Serve hot.

brussels sprouts & barley stew

If your child has only had Brussels sprouts with butter, she must try them like this. She'll find this rich, well-flavored stew hearty and satisfying.

SERVES:
4 adults and
4 children

PREPARATION TIME:
30 minutes, plus at least 7 hours soaking

COOKING TIME:
1 hour 40 minutes

STORAGE:
Refrigerate up to 3 days or freeze up to 3 months.

1 cup pearl barley
1 tbsp. kefir or plain yogurt
1 tbsp. olive oil
1 large onion, chopped
4 tomatoes, halved
4 cups trimmed and quartered lengthwise Brussels sprouts
3 tbsp. tamari
1 tbsp. vegetarian Worcestershire sauce

1 Put the barley and kefir in a large bowl, cover with warm water, and leave to soak, covered, 7 hours, or overnight, then drain.

2 Put the barley and 6 cups water in a very large saucepan and bring to a boil over high heat. Reduce the heat to low and simmer, covered, 45 minutes.

3 Heat the olive oil in a small saucepan over medium-high heat. Add the onion and cook 10 minutes, stirring occasionally, until soft and light brown. Make a small triangular cut at the stem-end of each tomato half to remove the hard part, then chop the tomatoes.

4 Add the onion, tomatoes, Brussels sprouts, tamari, and Worcestershire sauce to the barley and simmer, covered, 45 minutes longer, or until the barley is soft. Serve hot.

potato–parsnip pancakes

This twist on the classic potato pancake is a good way to incorporate parsnip into a new favorite for your little one.

SERVES:
2 adults and
2 children

PREPARATION TIME:
10 minutes

COOKING TIME:
18 minutes

STORAGE:
Not suitable for storage.

3 eggs
1 cup grated parsnip
1 cup grated potato
5 tbsp. wholegrain spelt flour
2 tbsp. butter

1 Put the eggs in a medium bowl and beat with a wire whisk, then mix in the parsnip, potato, and flour until blended.

2 Preheat the oven to 150°F. Melt the butter in a large skillet over medium-low heat, then drop tablespoonfuls of the parsnip mixture into the pan, spacing them well apart and flattening to ½ inch thick. Fry 3 minutes on each side until light brown and cooked through. Transfer to a plate and keep warm in the oven while you make the remaining pancakes. Serve warm.

parsnips are packed with healthy potassium, which helps regulate salt in the body. They're also an excellent source of dietary fibre and the antioxidant vitamin C.

(V) (Q) (X) (X)

baked mushroom open sandwich with tomato sauce

With crunchy bread and melting cheese, these excellently flavored warm sandwiches make a fabulous meal—one of Jessie's favorites. This recipe makes more tomato sauce than you will need for the sandwiches, but it's great to have on hand for quick meals.

SERVES:
2 adults and
2 children

PREPARATION
TIME:
30 minutes, plus at
least 1 hour chilling

COOKING TIME:
1 hour 50 minutes

STORAGE:
Refrigerate
the sauce up to
3 days or freeze
in portion-size jars
up to 3 months.
The sandwiches
are not suitable
for storage.

2 tbsp. olive oil, plus
   2 tsp. for frying
1 small onion, finely
   chopped
1⅔ cups brushed and
   chopped button
   mushrooms
½ cup black pitted olives,
   sliced
1 cup grated sharp
   cheddar cheese
2 garlic cloves, chopped
1 tsp. dried oregano
1 large wholewheat loaf
   of bread, sliced in half
   lengthwise

TOMATO SAUCE
2 tbsp. olive oil
2 large onions, chopped
1 red bell pepper, seeded
   and chopped
4 garlic cloves, chopped
3 bay leaves
2 tbsp. chopped parsley
½ tsp. dried thyme
1 tsp. dried oregano
1 tsp. dried basil
½ tsp. salt
3⅔ cups chopped
   tomatoes
2 cups tomato puree
6 tbsp. tomato paste

1 To make the tomato sauce, heat a large saucepan over medium-high heat. Add the oil and when it is hot, add the onion. Cook, stirring occasionally, 10 minutes, or until brown. Add the bell pepper and cook, stirring, 5 minutes longer, then stir in the remaining ingredients. Bring the mixture to a boil, then reduce the heat to low and simmer, covered, 1 hour, stirring occasionally.

2 When the sauce finishes cooking, heat 2 teaspoons of the olive oil in a small skillet over medium heat. Add the onion and cook, stirring occasionally, 10 minutes, or until soft. Remove from the heat.

3 Put the mushrooms, olives, cheddar, garlic, olive oil, and oregano in a medium bowl. Add the onion and 1⅓ cups of the tomato sauce and toss well. Cover and chill at least 1 hour.

4 Preheat the oven to 350°F. Remove some of the bread from the middle of each piece of bread to create a shallow hollow, then put the bread crust-side down on a cookie sheet. Spread each half generously with the mushroom sauce. Bake 30 minutes, or until the cheese melts, then slice and serve hot.

olives
are an excellent
source of vitamin E,
which helps protect cells
from oxidation. Green olives
are picked before they're
completely ripe, while black
olives are picked ripe.
Both are inedible until
cured in either brine
or oil.

pecan & stilton stuffed mushrooms

SERVES:
2 adults and
2 children

If your child likes stuffed mushrooms, she'll absolutely love these. Serve them with a big mixed salad and some fresh wholegrain bread for a deliciously satisfying meal.

PREPARATION TIME:
15 minutes

COOKING TIME:
30 minutes

STORAGE:
Not suitable
for storage.

6 large, flat field
   mushrooms (the larger
   and flatter, the better),
   brushed clean
2 tbsp. butter
1 large onion, finely
   chopped
¼ cup pecan halves,
   broken in half
   lengthwise (check
   for shell fragments)
2 slices of wholegrain
   spelt bread
1½ cups crumbled Stilton
   or other blue cheese
1 egg, beaten
4 tbsp. chopped parsley
1 lemon, cut into
   6 wedges

1 Preheat the broiler to medium. Carefully remove the stems from the mushrooms. Set the caps aside and finely chop the stems. Melt the butter in a medium skillet over medium-high heat, add the mushroom stems and onion, and cook 10 minutes, stirring occasionally, or until the onion is just soft.

2 Meanwhile, put the pecans in a baking dish and broil 2 to 3 minutes until light brown. Remove from the broiler and set aside.

3 Preheat the oven to 350°F. Lightly toast the bread, then put it in a blender. Blend 1 minute, or until bread crumbs form, then stir the bread crumbs, pecans, Stilton, egg, and parsley into the onion mixture.

4 Put the mushroom caps rounded-side down on a large cookie sheet and spoon the stuffing onto each one, dividing it equally among the six mushrooms. Bake 20 minutes, or until the mushrooms are cooked and sizzling and the filling is light brown. Squeeze the lemon wedges over the mushrooms and serve.

pecans
are super-rich in
good-quality oil. Because
they have a higher oil content
than most other nuts, they
go rancid more quickly, so
look for pale nuts when
you're shopping—the
paler, the fresher.

mediterranean wholewheat fusilli

SERVES:
2 adults and
2 children

PREPARATION
TIME:
15 minutes, plus
1 hour resting

COOKING TIME:
35 minutes

STORAGE:
Refrigerate
up to 3 days.

The vegetables in this recipe are cooked until they are soft and soupy, which is ideal when you're introducing your child to eggplant.

2½ cups peeled eggplant cut into ½in. cubes
1 tsp. salt, plus extra for cooking the pasta
3 tbsp. olive oil, plus extra for drizzling
1 large onion, chopped
1½ cups zucchini cut into ½in. cubes
3 garlic cloves, crushed
¾ cup vegetable broth
10½oz. dried wholewheat fusilli (spiral pasta)
¼ to ½ tsp. cayenne pepper (optional)

1 Put the eggplant in a colander, sprinkle with the salt, and leave to rest in the sink 1 hour.

2 Heat the olive oil in a large skillet over medium heat. Add the onion and cook 5 minutes, stirring occasionally, until beginning to soften. Reduce the heat to medium-low and add the eggplant, zucchini, tomatoes, garlic, and vegetable broth. Continue cooking, covered, over low heat 30 minutes, stirring occasionally, or until the vegetables are cooked.

3 When the vegetables are almost finished cooking, bring a large pan of salted water to a boil and cook the pasta according to the package directions, then drain and return it to the pan.

4 Drizzle the pasta with a little olive oil and toss well, then divide it into four bowls. Spoon several tablespoons of the vegetable mixture over each child portion. Mix the cayenne pepper, if using, into the remaining vegetables and spoon it over the adult portions. Serve immediately.

onions
contain quercetin and chromium, powerful compounds that maintain a good hormone balance and protect the immune system. They also carry natural prebiotic fiber that stimulate the growth and function of probiotics.

curried rice with cranberries & almonds

SERVES:
2 adults and
2 children

PREPARATION
TIME:
10 minutes,
plus at least
7 hours
soaking

COOKING TIME:
30 minutes

STORAGE:
Refrigerate up
to 1 day. Reheat
until hot.

Here's a way to introduce tart cranberries to your child in a savory dish. It also includes almonds, one of the healthiest nuts, which provide protein and good-quality fat. Here, they're toasted to add a nutty crunchiness.

1 cup brown basmati rice
1 tbsp. kefir or plain yogurt
⅓ cup dried cranberries
1 tbsp. olive oil
1 small onion, finely chopped
½ cup whole shelled almonds with skins
1 tbsp. curry powder
⅛ tsp. cayenne pepper

1 Put the rice, kefir, and 2 cups warm water in a medium saucepan and leave to soak, covered, 7 hours, or overnight.

2 Bring the rice to a boil over high heat, then reduce the heat to low and cook, covered, 30 minutes, or until the rice is just tender.

3 While the rice is cooking, put the cranberries in a small bowl, cover with 4 tablespoons warm water, and leave to soak 15 minutes, then drain.

4 Meanwhile, preheat the broiler to medium. Heat the olive oil in a small skillet over medium heat until hot. Add the onion and cook 10 minutes, stirring occasionally, or until soft.

5 Put the almonds on a cookie sheet and broil 3 minutes, or until light brown.

6 Put the rice, cranberries, onion, almonds, curry powder, and cayenne pepper in a medium bowl and toss well. Serve warm.

almonds
are, gram for gram, the most nutritionally dense nut. They are high in vitamin E and their skins contain flavanoid antioxidants, which makes a great combination. Keep the skins on to give your child the best nutritional kick possible.

make-your-own sushi

Cook the rice, chop the vegetables, put it all on the table, and your job is done! Letting your kids assemble their own sushi rolls is a great way to get them involved with their food—and it makes them feel grown up.

PREPARATION
TIME:
15 minutes, plus
at least 7 hours
soaking

COOKING TIME:
30 minutes

STORAGE:
Refrigerate the
rice up to 1 day.
Reheat until hot.

1 cup brown basmati rice
1 tbsp. kefir or plain
  yogurt
1 small piece horseradish
  root, peeled and finely
  grated, or 3 to 4 tbsp.
  bottled horseradish
  sauce
3 to 4 tbsp. mayonnaise,
  plus extra as needed
  (optional)
12 sheets of nori, cut in
  half crosswise
1 cucumber, cut into thin
  matchsticks
2 carrots, cut into thin
  matchsticks
1 avocado, halved, pitted,
  peeled, and cut into
  strips
3oz. alfalfa sprouts
umeboshi paste
wasabi paste

1 Put the rice, kefir, and 2 cups warm water in a medium saucepan and leave to soak, covered, 7 hours, or overnight.

2 Bring the rice to a boil over high heat, reduce the heat to low, and cook, covered, 30 minutes, or until the rice is just tender.

3 While the rice is cooking, divide the grated horseradish root, if using, into two small bowls and mix with the mayonnaise. For adults, use equal amounts of horseradish and mayonnaise; for children use 1 part horseradish to 3 parts mayonnaise. If using a bottled horseradish sauce, simply put the sauce in a small serving bowl. Put the sauce on the table.

4 Set the other components of the sushi on the table: Put the nori sheets on two plates and divide the cucumber, carrots, and avocado onto two additional plates. Divide the sprouts into two small bowls and put the umeboshi paste and wasabi paste in separate ramekins or small bowls. Divide the rice into two serving bowls.

5 Show everyone how to make their own sushi—and give the family chef a break—although a two-year-old might need some help. To assemble the sushi, put 1 piece of nori, shiny-side down, on a plate. Spread a very thin strip of the umeboshi and wasabi pastes along the bottom of the nori—both are very strong in flavor. Then spread some of the horseradish sauce over, followed by 2 tablespoons of the rice. Top with 1 to 3 strips of vegetables and some sprouts, then roll the sushi upward to form a log. It might not be as tidy as in the picture at right, but it will still be delicious. Eat immediately.

umeboshi
**is a fermented
Japanese plum. Its
powerful acidity has an
alkalizing effect on the
body. It combats tiredness,
stimulates digestion,
and promotes the
elimination
of toxins.**

◄ noodles with vegetables

SERVES:
2 adults and
2 children

PREPARATION
TIME:
15 minutes

COOKING TIME:
15 minutes

STORAGE:
Not suitable
for storage.

Miso, a fermented soy food, is one of the world's most medicinal foods. Keep some in the refrigerator and get in the habit of adding it to soups and sauces.

10oz. udon noodles
2 cups carrots cut into
1½in.-long matchsticks
2 cups zucchini cut into
1½in.-long matchsticks
4 tbsp. mellow brown
miso
3 tbsp. tahini
2 tbsp. brown rice vinegar
1 tbsp. mirin
1 garlic clove, chopped
4 scallions, thinly sliced,
to serve
salt

1 Bring a large saucepan of salted water to a boil and cook the udon noodles according to the package directions, then drain.

2 While the noodles are cooking, put the carrots in a steamer and steam, covered, over boiling water 2 minutes. Add the zucchini to the carrots and steam 4 minutes longer, or until just soft.

3 Put the miso and tahini in a small saucepan and stir over low heat until smooth. Add 5 tablespoons water and stir until smooth. Add the brown rice vinegar, mirin, and garlic and heat until warm.

4 Divide the noodles into four bowls and divide the steamed vegetables over the noodles. Top each portion with about 4 tablespoons of the sauce. Sprinkle with the scallions and serve hot.

potato & egg salad

SERVES:
2 adults and
4 as a main dish

PREPARATION
TIME:
15 minutes

COOKING TIME:
15 minutes

STORAGE:
Refrigerate
up to 2 days.

This fantastic potato salad, livened up by vinegar and crisp vegetables, is excellent freshly made and warm—or chilled and taken on a picnic.

3 cups unpeeled potatoes
cut into ¾in. cubes
4 eggs, at room
temperature
1 small onion, finely
chopped
2 garlic cloves, finely
chopped
1 red bell pepper, seeded
and chopped
2 celery sticks, chopped
½ cup mayonnaise
4 tbsp. white wine
vinegar

1 Put the potatoes in steamer and steam, covered, over boiling water 15 minutes, or until just soft. Remove from the heat and leave to cool.

2 Meanwhile, pierce the large end of each egg with a pin. Bring a medium saucepan of water to a boil, add the eggs, and cook 9 minutes. Remove from the heat, drain the water from the pan and refill with cold water to cover the eggs. Leave until cool enough to handle, then drain. Peel the eggs, then quarter them lengthwise and cut into bite-size chunks.

3 Put the eggs in a large bowl and add the potatoes, onion, garlic, red bell pepper, celery, mayonnaise, and vinegar and mix well. Serve at room temperature or chilled.

toasted quinoa & vegetable salad

SERVES:
2 adults and
2 children

PREPARATION
TIME:
20 minutes

COOKING TIME:
35 minutes

STORAGE:
Refrigerate
up to 3 days
but don't reheat.
Serve cold or at
room temperature.

This colorful, nutrient-packed salad is perfect for kids—Cassie absolutely loves it—and it's incredibly versatile: you can use any combination of finely chopped vegetables to cater to your child's growing tastes.

½ cup quinoa
½ cup broccoli florets cut into tiny pieces
juice of ½ lemon
1 tbsp. olive oil
1 tbsp. tahini
1 carrot, grated
½ yellow bell pepper, seeded and finely chopped
1 cup finely chopped cucumber
4 small scallions, thinly sliced
¼ cup alfalfa sprouts

1 Put the quinoa in a strainer and rinse under cold running water, then drain well. Transfer to a medium saucepan and toast over high heat 5 minutes, stirring continuously, or until any excess water evaporates and the quinoa is lightly brown and beginning to pop.

2 Add 1 cup water and bring to a boil over high heat. Reduce the heat to low and simmer, covered, 30 minutes, or until tender. Remove from the heat and leave to cool.

3 Shortly before the quinoa finishes cooking, put the broccoli in a steamer and steam, covered, over boiling water 3 minutes, or until tender. Meanwhile, put the lemon juice, olive oil, and tahini in a small bowl and mix well, then set aside.

4 Transfer the broccoli to a medium bowl and add the quinoa, carrot, yellow bell pepper, cucumber, scallions, and alfalfa sprouts and toss together. When ready to serve, pour the dressing over the vegetables, mix well, and serve.

tahini
is rich in essential oils
that support healthy brain
and nerve development. It has
lots of iron and B vitamins,
which contribute to healthy cell
growth, and it's a good source
of methionine, an amino
acid that keeps the
liver healthy.

hot sardine toasts

SERVES:
2 adults and
2 children

PREPARATION
TIME:
10 minutes

COOKING TIME:
40 minutes

STORAGE:
Not suitable
for storage.

I could eat plain sardines until the cows come home, but if I ever feel like a change, this is the dish I crave. The creamy sauce paired with the piquant gherkins and capers make this dish especially appealing to children.

2 tbsp. butter
1 tbsp. all-purpose flour
½ cup milk
⅓ cup mayonnaise
1 tbsp. finely chopped pitted green olives
2 tbsp. finely chopped gherkin
2 tbsp. finely chopped onion
2 tsp. small capers
½ tsp. cider vinegar
6 slices of wholewheat bread
12oz. canned sardines, drained

1 Put the butter in the top of a double boiler or in a medium bowl resting over a pan of boiling water. Stir in the flour, then add the milk and mayonnaise, stirring until smooth. Continue stirring continuously 30 minutes longer, or until a thick sauce forms. Remove from the heat and mix in the olives, gherkin, onion, capers, and vinegar.

2 Preheat the broiler to medium. While the broiler is heating, toast the bread in a toaster and put it on a cookie sheet. Cover each slice of toast with the sardines. If the sardines are large, mash them onto the bread so you have a layer of sardines. Spoon about 3 tablespoons of the sauce over the sardines and broil 3 to 4 minutes until hot and the sauce is bubbling. Serve immediately.

haddock with capers

SERVES:
2 adults and
2 children

PREPARATION
TIME:
10 minutes

COOKING TIME:
20 minutes

STORAGE:
Refrigerate
up to 1 day.

Nicholas loves this easy and delicious baked fish. The pretty cherry tomatoes and little green capers will catch your child's interest, and letting her squeeze her own lemon will make her feel more grown up.

olive oil, for greasing
14oz. skinned haddock fillet, cut into 4 pieces
4 tsp. capers
4 cherry tomatoes, quartered lengthwise
1 lemon, cut into 4 wedges
salt

1 Preheat the oven to 300°F and grease a medium baking dish with olive oil. Put the fish pieces in the dish, sprinkle lightly with salt and put 1 teaspoon of the capers and four pieces of tomato on each piece.

2 Bake 20 minutes, or until the fish is white. Squeeze 1 lemon wedge over each piece of fish and serve hot.

lemons are an excellent source of vitamin C, which is vital for a strong immune system. When added to foods, fresh lemon juice lifts the flavor and adds zing.

▼ shrimp pasta bake

I always use yogurt instead of cream when I can because it's so much healthier, especially for little ones.

SERVES:
2 adults and
2 children

PREPARATION TIME:
10 minutes

COOKING TIME:
40 minutes

STORAGE:
Refrigerate
up to 2 days.

¼ tsp. salt, plus extra for cooking the pasta
2 cups dried wholewheat pasta, such as elbows or shells
10oz. raw shelled shrimp, cut into bite-size pieces
scant 1 cup plain yogurt
½ tsp. dried herbes de Provence
2 tbsp. chopped parsley

1 Preheat the oven to 350°F and bring a large saucepan of salted water to a boil. Cook the pasta 2 minutes less than the package directions suggest, then remove from the heat, drain, and return to the pan.

2 Mix in the shrimp, yogurt, herbes de Provence, parsley, and salt and transfer the mixture to a deep baking dish, about 7 x 7 inches. Bake 30 minutes until the shrimp are cooked and the pasta is heated through, then serve.

▼ chicken with apricot & fennel wild rice

Wild rice is not technically rice: it's an aquatic cereal grass native to North America. Delicious on its own, it also makes a great stuffing.

SERVES:
2 adults and
2 children

PREPARATION TIME:
15 minutes, plus at least 7 hours soaking

COOKING TIME:
40 minutes

STORAGE:
Refrigerate the rice and chicken up to 1 day. Reheat the rice until hot.

¾ cup wild rice
1 tbsp. kefir or plain yogurt
5 tbsp. plus 2 tsp. olive oil
4 chicken boneless, skinless chicken breast halves, about 3½oz. each, cut into strips
6 apricots, pitted and diced
⅓ cup finely chopped fennel
½ tsp. salt

1 Put the rice, kefir, and 2 cups warm water in a medium saucepan and soak, covered, 7 hours, or overnight.

2 Bring to a boil over high heat, then reduce the heat to low and simmer, covered, 40 minutes, or until the rice is just soft. Shortly before the rice finishes cooking, heat 2 teaspoons of the olive oil in a medium skillet over medium heat until hot. Put the chicken in the pan and cook 5 minutes on each side until light brown and cooked through.

3 Transfer the rice to a serving bowl. Mix in the apricots, fennel, salt, and remaining olive oil and serve warm with the chicken.

pork with gherkins

SERVES:
2 adults and
2 children

PREPARATION
TIME:
15 minutes,
plus overnight
soaking

COOKING TIME:
1 hour 10 minutes

STORAGE:
Refrigerate
up to 2 days.
This tastes even
better the day
after it is made.

We were all a bit skeptical when my mom first made this dish, and then we were surprised by how much we loved it—especially when it was reheated the next day.

1 cup brown basmati rice
1 tbsp. kefir or plain yogurt
4 pork chops, about 2lb.
3 tbsp. butter
1 large onion, chopped
⅓ cup red wine vinegar
1 large tomato, diced
2 tbsp. tomato paste
1 tbsp. chopped parsley
½ tsp. dried thyme
½ tsp. dried tarragon
2 tbsp. Dijon mustard
½ cup sliced gherkins
salt

1 Put the rice, kefir, and 2 cups warm water in a medium saucepan and leave to soak, covered, 7 hours, or overnight.

2 Sprinkle the pork chops with salt. Melt 11 tablespoon of the butter in a large, heavy skillet over medium-high heat, then add the pork chops and cook 5 minutes on each side until brown. Remove from the heat and transfer the chops to a platter.

3 Add the remaining tablespoon butter to the skillet and melt over medium heat. Add the onion and cook 5 minutes, stirring occasionally, until beginning to brown. Add half of the vinegar and simmer until most of it evaporates. Stir in the tomato, tomato paste, parsley, thyme, tarragon, and 1 cup water, then return chops to the pan and simmer, covered, 45 minutes, or until tender.

4 Meanwhile, bring the rice to a boil over high heat, then reduce the heat to low, cover, and cook 30 minutes, or until just tender. Remove from the heat and set aside.

5 Add the mustard, gherkins, and remaining vinegar to the chops and mix well. Cook, covered, 10 minutes longer, then serve, spooning the sauce over the rice and cutting the chops into smaller pieces for the child portions.

herbs & spices
bring flavor and health to our foods whether they are used fresh or dried. Depending on the type, herbs and spices can help to strengthen the immune system and fight infection. Many are antibacterial and antifungal, too.

muesli cookies

My kids love these very nutritious, very delicious cookies. The sesame seeds add a lovely toasty flavor, while the raisins and apricots add a sweet chewiness.

MAKES:
About 80 cookies

PREPARATION
TIME:
30 minutes

COOKING TIME:
45 minutes

STORAGE:
Store in an airtight container at room temperature up to 5 days.

1 cup plus 2 tbsp.
  (2¼ sticks) butter,
  softened
¾ cup brown rice syrup
1 egg
1 tsp. vanilla extract
2½ cups wholegrain spelt
  flour
½ tsp. baking powder
1 cup rolled oats
½ cup quinoa flakes
½ cup millet flakes
½ cup sunflower seeds
⅓ cup sesame seeds
⅔ cup raisins
⅔ cup finely chopped
  unsulfured dried
  apricots
⅓ cup chocolate chips
  (optional)

1 Preheat the oven to 350°F. Put the butter, brown rice syrup, egg, vanilla extract, and ½ cup water in a large bowl and beat, using an electric mixer on medium speed or by hand using a whisk or wooden spoon, 10 minutes, or until creamy.

2 In a medium bowl, mix together the flour, baking powder, oats, quinoa flakes, millet flakes, sunflower seeds, sesame seeds, raisins, apricots, and chocolate chips, if using. Add the dry mixture to the wet mixture and stir with a wooden spoon until blended.

3 Working in batches, drop 20 teaspoonfuls of the dough onto a cookie sheet, spacing them ¾ inch apart. Bake 11 minutes, or until light brown. Remove from the oven and, using a spatula, transfer the cookies to a wire rack and leave to cool. Serve warm or at room temperature.

seeds
are high in nutrients such as iron, vitamin E, and essential fatty acids. They are the "eggs" that hold everything necessary to nourish a new plant. We should eat these nutritional wonders regularly, not only as the occasional snack.

date, oat & hazelnut bars

Moist, dense, and filling, these bars are great for a mid-morning or afternoon snack when your child wants something sweet. They're also easy to take out and about, so you always have a healthy snack to hand.

MAKES:
9 bars

PREPARATION TIME:
15 minutes, plus 10 minutes soaking

COOKING TIME:
1 hour 5 minutes

STORAGE:
Store in an airtight container at room temperature up to 2 days and then refrigerate up to 3 days.

½ cup hazelnuts
5 tbsp. butter, melted, plus extra for greasing
1½ cups rolled oats
½ cup chopped dried dates
¼ cup brown rice syrup
1 egg, beaten
1 tsp. vanilla extract
½ cup wholegrain spelt flour
1 tsp. cinnamon
½ tsp. baking powder

1 Heat the broiler to medium. Put the hazelnuts on a small baking tray and broil 3 minutes, or until beginning to brown. Remove from the heat and leave to cool.

2 Preheat oven to 350°F and grease an 8- x 8-inch baking pan with butter. Put the oats and dates in a bowl, stir in 1½ cups warm water, and leave to soak 10 minutes. Meanwhile, put the cool hazelnuts in a plastic bag and pound them with a rolling pin or bottle until crushed, then add them to the oats.

3 Add the brown rice syrup, butter, egg, and vanilla extract to the oats and mix well.

4 In another bowl, mix together the flour, cinnamon, and baking powder, then add it to the oat mixture and mix well, using a wooden spoon or rubber spatula.

5 Pour the batter into the baking pan, smoothing the top with the back of the spoon. Bake 1 hour, or until light brown. Remove from the oven and leave to cool slightly, then cut into 9 squares. Serve warm or at room temperature.

brown rice syrup
is a naturally malted whole-grain sweetener. The highest-quality sweetener available, it is made by a slow, natural enzymatic process in which the grains of brown rice are broken down to yield a thick, sweet, rich liquid.

blueberry loaf

Blueberries are one of nature's wonderfoods and add nutrition to everything they're used in. Eat them raw, make a pie, or bake with them. You can serve this quickbread as a delicious breakfast, a great afternoon snack, or a delightful dessert that children will adore.

MAKES:
1 loaf

PREPARATION TIME:
20 minutes

COOKING TIME:
1 hour 5 minutes

STORAGE:
Store in an airtight container up to 2 days and then refrigerate up to 3 days.

½ cup (1 stick) butter, softened, plus extra for greasing
1 cup white spelt flour, plus extra for flouring
½ cup sugar
2 eggs
1 cup wholegrain spelt flour
1 tsp. baking powder
½ cup rice milk
2 cups blueberries

1 Preheat the oven to 350°F and grease and flour a 9- x 4-inch bread pan. Put the butter and sugar in a large bowl and beat, using an electric mixer, at medium speed 10 minutes, or until light and fluffy. Add the eggs, one at a time, beating well after each one.

2 In a medium bowl, combine the flours and baking powder. Add half of the flour mixture to the butter mixture and beat at low speed until just mixed, then beat in the rice milk followed by the remaining flour, beating until just blended. Fold in the blueberries, using a rubber spatula, and spoon the batter into the bread pan.

3 Bake 1 hour 5 minutes, or until light brown, cracked in the middle, and just pulling away from the sides of the pan. A toothpick inserted into the middle should come out clean. Remove from the oven and leave to cool in the pan on a wire rack 15 minutes, then run a knife along the sides of the pan and turn the loaf out onto the wire rack to cool completely. Serve warm or at room temperature.

blueberries
are packed with vitamin C and vitamin E, making them one of the most antioxidant-rich of all fruit and vegetables. They're great for healthy cell growth and for maintaining healthy cholesterol levels.

independence days

It probably seems like all you did was blink, and your baby turned into a walking, talking, independent little person with aspirations and opinions of his own. If you've followed the advice in this book, he's also developed a love of good food, so continue giving him nutritious meals whenever you can. He's experiencing more of the world on his own now and forming friendships—some of which might last a lifetime. Parties and picnics are a great chance for him to socialize with other kids and share food. From simple dishes like Guacamole and Chickpea Pancakes to indulgent treats such as Cream Cheese & Salmon Blinis and Spelt Cake, the choices are plentiful, and you don't have to spend weeks planning. The lunchbox ideas here will help to ensure he eats well at school, too.

Mini Pita Pizzas (see page 154)

4 to 5 years

Your child will now be spending more time away from you at other people's houses, playgroups, parties, and school or kindergarten. This means he will experience other foods and ways of eating. Continue with the good eating habits you've established at home. This book is not about eating perfectly; it's about creating good habits so your child eats really well most of the time. Then you don't have to worry about the rest of the time.

The recipes here are for picnics, lunchboxes, and parties, and are organized in that order. Of course, they can be incorporated into your regular cooking, too. Many are great for light lunches at home, and the cake is perfect for birthdays and other special occasions.

I hope by now you're feeling confident about cooking and have realized it isn't some mysterious art. You might think some of these recipes would be better with a little more or a little less of something. Start recreating some of your favorites by swapping vegetables, changing ingredient proportions, or simply omitting an item you don't like. The recipes aren't fixed in stone, so make them your own ... well, except the ones passed down to me by my mom. Those, of course, are sacred, so don't mess with them.

Picnics

I love picnics. If you've got a good supply of food and drink, you can stay outside for a long time. The recipes in this section are all easy to prepare and portable. Supplement them with jars of olives, gherkins, sun-dried tomatoes, broiled artichoke hearts, and roasted garlic. Meat and veggie sausages can be cooked beforehand and served warm or at room temperature, so bring little containers of mustard and ketchup for dipping. For kids, you can add raw cucumber "coins" and carrot sticks and a pack of grissini. A selection of cheeses, crackers, organic chocolate, a bottle each of water and wine, and a thermos of jasmine tea, are great additions to round off the perfect spread.

In addition to plates, silverware, and cups, you'll need a board for cheese, a small sharp knife, a corkscrew, paper towels, rubbish bags, hand wipes, spare clothes, sweaters, sunscreen, homeopathic remedies for bug and bee stings, bandages, a blanket, a ball, and some toys. Pray for sun, head somewhere pretty, and have some fun!

Lunchboxes

I think lunches for school must be easy enough to make in the morning. Even with only one child, I don't think you want to be preparing more food at the end of the day after you have cleaned up the kitchen for the last time and could be spending time with your partner or simply enjoying some down time. Every lunchbox menu here can be thrown together in about 20 minutes. You just need a few things you can defrost from the freezer the night before, like pesto or pasta sauce. To make life easier, I steam a batch of vegetables to last for a couple of days, so I don't have to cook them for every meal—and I use these for making lunches in the morning.

Again, variety is the key. Many children don't want a lot of any one thing at lunch (not even a whole sandwich), so a wide selection of foods increases the chances he'll eat a better, more balanced meal. Remember, you're not there to help and encourage him over lunch any more, so make his lunchbox something he'll look forward to each day.

Parties

Your child will be going to parties and will be exposed to an amazing range of foods, some new and wonderful, and some absolute junk. I don't want to create issues around food, so I let my kids eat what they want at parties. I do, however, remind them that this is not how we eat at home or every day, and I ask them to notice how they feel. It's meaningless to tell a child that something is bad for him, especially if you say it repeatedly. Instead, teach him to notice how food makes him feel physically, especially his tummy or head. I talked to Jessie about this when she was a toddler, just before she put a very sweet chocolatey thing in her mouth. She listened, ate it, and then came back to me a few minutes later and said, "Oh, I'm all dizzy and spinny" (because of the sugar and caffeine). Don't think all of your efforts are wasted once your child leaves the house, either. Even if kids do rebel at some point, after a while they usually go back to what they knew before.

The party menus on page 141 provide a nice combination of cold, warm, and finger foods that are great for parties. Each menu includes a few very quick and easy dishes, as well as foods that can be made in advance, which makes planning and executing the food for the party easier. All of the recipes are packed with good, nutritious ingredients, and they also have a whimsical element so kids will find them fun to eat. Finger foods such as Mini Pitta Pizzas, Cream Cheese & Salmon Blinis and Cherry Tomatoes with Hummus & Capers, for example, are always popular.

Because I serve sweets and desserts so rarely, I like to do something really special for birthdays and festive occasions. The cake recipe on page 159 is especially great for kids. Not only does it taste delicious, but it also provides nutrition because about half of the flour is wholegrain spelt flour. If you decorate it with cut fruit, which can be quite pretty, you avoid a sugary frosting, too. The cake is also easy to handle when you want to transfer it to a pretty serving plate or for cutting into interesting shapes. I've made it into everything from a spaceship to a fairy castle.

If you're planning a party for a four- or five-year old, six is the ideal number of guests—unless you want to invite the whole class. Allow two hours, usually 3:00 to 5:00 in the afternoon. Have someone who is close to your child there to help out. Start with some sort of art activity and have your helper run some games while you set the table.

MEAL PLANNER: LUNCHBOXES

A varied menu helps to liven up your child's lunch and keep him interested in his food. A small juice box makes a nice occasional treat in addition to water.

MONDAY	TUESDAY	WEDNESDAY	THURSDAY	FRIDAY
Cheddar & Watercress Sandwich (see page 149)	Spelt Pasta with Pesto (see page 148)	Lemon–Mackerel, Mayo & Cucumber Sandwiches (see page 104)	Corn Pasta with Tomato Sauce (see page 148)	Hemp Seed & Egg Salad Sandwich (see page 150)
celery sticks and broccoli florets	Cucumber & Tomato Salad (see page 151)	Carrot & Pea Salad (see page 151)	Arugula & Lemon Salad (see page 150)	cauliflower florets and red bell pepper
blueberries	½ apple, sliced and sprinkled with lemon juice	grapes	½ banana (skin on)	unsulfured dried apricots
seeds and nori squares	plain yogurt	water	almonds	rice cakes
water	water		water	water

For variety other weeks, try substituting some of the above with the following:

SUBSTITUTE ...	WITH ...
vegetables	asparagus, avocado (must be sprinkled with lemon), raw zucchini slices, fennel, green beans, snow peas, sugar snap peas, raw or cooked turnip slices, rutabaga, and so on
unsulfured dried apricots	dried cranberries, dates, figs, dried mango, pineapple, prunes, raisins, golden raisins, and so on
rice cakes	corn cakes, oatcakes, rye crispbreads, Japanese brown rice crackers, wholegrain spelt, wholewheat grissini and/or pretzels, and so on
fruit	other berries, clementines, kiwi, orange segments, satsumas, and so on
almonds	Brazil nuts, hazelnuts, macadamia nuts, pecans, pine nuts, pistachio nuts, and walnuts

Present each food on two plates, one at each end of the table, so that all the kids can easily reach everything. At 4:00, it's time to eat. After that, have the birthday star open presents with all of the children gathered around. Have your helper keep a list of who gave what in order to avoid confusion when writing thank-you notes. In the meantime, you can get the table ready for everyone's favorite moment: the cake. Around 4:30, it's time for singing, candles, and cake. Afterward, play another game or take everyone outside to play, if the weather allows, until the parents arrive to collect the children. You can also invite the parents to come a little earlier for cake and just cut it into smaller pieces.

PARTY MENUS (FOR 8 CHILDREN)

Although you can mix and match the ten party recipes in this chapter any way you like, the two menus below are ones I often use.

MENU 1	QUANTITY PER CHILD	PREPARATION TIME (IN MINUTES)	COOKING TIME (IN MINUTES)
Sesame & Raisin Bread Balls (see page 153)	2	30	30
Cherry Tomatoes with Hummus & Capers (see page 154)	3 or 4	20	–
Chickpea Pancakes (see page 152)	1 or 2	10	10
Cheesy Polenta Bites (see page 156)	4	10	20
Sweet Potato Fish Balls (see page 157)	3	15	25
Spelt Cake (see page 159)			
TOTAL	13 to 15	85	75

MENU 2	QUANTITY PER CHILD	PREPARATION TIME (IN MINUTES)	COOKING TIME (IN MINUTES)
Cherry Tomatoes with Hummus & Capers (see page 154)	3 or 4	20	–
Cream Cheese & Salmon Blinis (see page 157)	4 or 5	15	20
Mini Pita Pizzas (see page 154)	1	10	5
Sweet Potato & Carrot Patties (see page 155)	1 or 2	15	35
Tofu Squares (see page 156)	3	10	5
Spelt Cake (see page 159)			
TOTAL	12 to 15	70	65

wholegrain spelt bread

MAKES:
1 large loaf

Making your own bread is so satisfying, and this dense, moist loaf is proof it's also easy—and doesn't require a bread machine.

PREPARATION TIME:
20 minutes,
plus 3 to 48 hours
rising

COOKING TIME:
30 minutes

STORAGE:
Store the baked bread in an airtight container up to 4 days. The dough can be made to the end of step 1 and frozen (all or half) up to 3 months in an airtight plastic bag. To bake, put the dough on a greased cookie sheet, leave to come to room temperature, and then rise 1 hour. Then bake as in step 5.

long fermentation
with kefir or yogurt allows the phytic acid, hard-to-digest proteins, and complex starches in the flour to break down. This method also increases vitamin content and makes the nutrients in the grains more available for absorption.

2 tsp. olive oil, plus oil for greasing
5½ cups wholegrain spelt flour
1 tbsp. active dry yeast
1 tbsp. salt
1 tbsp. kefir or plain yogurt
butter, for greasing

1 Grease a medium bowl with olive oil and set aside. In a large bowl, mix together the flour, yeast, and salt. Add the olive oil, kefir, and 1½ cups plus 2 tablespoons lukewarm water. Mix with your hands until it nearly all comes together, adding an extra 1 to 2 tablespoons water, if necessary. Pour the contents of the bowl onto the countertop and knead by stretching the dough away from you, then gathering it back, turning it 90 degrees and repeating, incorporating in all the flour as you knead. The dough might seem a little dry at first, but the ingredients will come together as you work it. Knead 10 minutes, or until it is smooth and elastic. If the dough is sticking to your hands, add a little more flour a bit at a time; if it is too dry for the dry ingredients to come together, add a little more water.

2 Transfer the dough to the oiled bowl, rubbing a little olive oil over the surface of the dough. Put a clean, damp dish towel on the surface of the dough so it doesn't dry out and form a crust, and chill 24 hours. Alternatively, if you don't want to wait for a long fermentation and want to bake the loaf on the same day, leave the covered dough to rise at room temperature 1½ to 2 hours until it doubles in size, then skip step 3 and go directly to step 4.

3 Take the dough out of the refrigerator and punch it down thoroughly to get all the air out. Turn it onto the countertop, knead 1 minute, shape into a ball, and put it back in the bowl. Cover again with the damp dish towel and return it to the refrigerator 24 hours longer.

4 Grease a cookie sheet with butter and set aside. Turn the dough out onto the countertop and punch down thoroughly. Knead 1 minute, then shape it into a ball and put it on the cookie sheet. Cover with the damp tea towel again and leave to rise at room temperature 1 to 1½ hours until double in size.

5 Preheat the oven to 425°F. Remove the dish towel and put the bread in the oven. Bake 10 minutes, then reduce the oven temperature to 375° and bake 20 minutes longer, or until the loaf is golden brown and sounds hollow when tapped. Remove from the oven and leave to cool on a wire rack 15 minutes. Serve warm or at room temperature.

adzuki–yogurt dip

SERVES:
8

PREPARATION TIME:
10 minutes, plus overnight soaking

COOKING TIME:
55 minutes

STORAGE:
Refrigerate up to 2 days.

A few dips are always a good idea at a picnic, and this one is a nice change from hummus. It's mild, smooth, and creamy—and a pretty pink color.

1 cup dried adzuki beans
6 tsp. lemon juice
1 strip of kombu, about 6 x 2in.
½ cup Greek-style yogurt
1 tsp. ground cumin
1 tsp. salt
vegetable sticks (optional), to serve
tortilla chips (optional), to serve

1 Put the beans and 2 teaspoons of the lemon juice in a medium saucepan, cover with warm water, and leave to soak, covered, overnight.

2 Drain and rinse the beans. Return them to the pan and add 3¼ cups water. Bring to a boil over high heat and boil 10 minutes, skimming any scum that rises to the surface. Reduce the heat to low, add the kombu, and cook, covered, 45 minutes, or until the beans are soft. The beans should remain covered with water, so add extra boiled water during cooking, if necessary. Then drain and leave to cool.

3 Put the beans and kombu, yogurt, cumin, salt, and remaining lemon juice in a blender. Blend 1 minute, or until smooth, then serve with vegetable sticks and/or tortilla chips.

egg salad

SERVES:
8

PREPARATION TIME:
15 minutes

COOKING TIME:
9 minutes

STORAGE:
Refrigerate up to 2 days.

This is the egg salad I grew up with—a wonderful variation of the classic recipe. It's a great dish for picnics because it's so portable. You can eat it by itself or spread it on crackers or bread.

6 eggs, at room temperature
2 large gherkins, diced
1 small red onion, finely chopped
1 garlic clove, chopped
2 tbsp. chopped parsley
⅛ tsp. salt
2 tbsp. mayonnaise
2 tbsp. non-hot mustard

1 Pierce the large end of each egg with a pin. Bring a medium saucepan of water to a boil and, using a spoon, carefully put the eggs in the water. Boil 9 minutes, then remove from the heat, drain the hot water from the pan and refill it with cold water to cool the eggs and stop them cooking. Set aside until cool enough to handle.

2 Peel the eggs, put them in a medium bowl, and mash with a fork or potato masher. Add the gherkins, onion, garlic, parsley, salt, mayonnaise, and mustard and mix well. Serve at room temperature or chilled.

▼ guacamole

SERVES:
8

PREPARATION
TIME:
15 minutes

STORAGE:
Refrigerate
up to 3 days.

I'm always surprised at how quickly two avocados disappear at a picnic when there's always so much other food. Jessie, especially, gives this winning recipe an enthusiastic thumbs up every time.

2 avocados, halved and pitted
1 tomato, finely chopped
juice of 1 lemon
¼ tsp. salt
⅛ tsp. hot-pepper sauce
vegetable sticks (optional), to serve

1 Scoop the avocado flesh into a medium bowl and mash using a fork, leaving it a bit lumpy.

2 Add the tomato, lemon juice, salt, and hot-pepper and mix well. Serve chilled or at room temperature.

marinated cauliflower

SERVES:
8

PREPARATION TIME:
10 minutes, plus 20 minutes marinating

COOKING TIME:
5 minutes

STORAGE:
Keep at room temperature in a covered bowl up to 4 hours.

This surprisingly simple and delicious way to serve cauliflower appeals to children and adults alike.

3 cups bite-size cauliflower florets
4 tbsp. olive oil
2 tbsp. brown rice vinegar

1 Put the cauliflower in a steamer and steam, covered, over boiling water 5 minutes, or until just tender.

2 Transfer the cauliflower to a medium serving bowl and, while it's still warm, drizzle the olive oil and vinegar over. Toss well and then leave to marinate at room temperature at least 20 minutes while you pack your picnic things or travel to the picnic. Serve at room temperature

brown rice vinegar is treasured for its mellow flavor and light sweetness. The best kind is made in the traditional Japanese way, with only fermented sweet brown rice and water.

parsley pesto & penne

SERVES:
8

PREPARATION TIME:
15 minutes

COOKING TIME:
10 minutes

STORAGE:
Refrigerate the pesto up to 3 days or freeze up to 3 months.

Pesto, with its toasty pine nuts, fresh herbs, pungent garlic, and quality olive oil, is heaven with pasta. This recipe uses parsley instead of basil  and is made without cheese.

⅓ cup pine nuts
¾ tsp. salt, plus extra for cooking the pasta
4 cups dried wholewheat penne pasta
2 cups chopped parsley
3 garlic cloves, crushed
½ cup olive oil

1 Preheat the broiler to medium. Put the pine nuts in a flameproof dish and broil 1 minute, or until toasted, watching carefully so they do not burn. Remove from the broiler and set aside.

2 Bring a large saucepan of salted water to a boil. Add the pasta and cook according to the package directions, then drain and transfer to a large bowl.

3 While the pasta is cooking, put the pine nuts, parsley, garlic, salt, and olive oil in a blender and blend 1 minute, or until smooth.

4 Pour the pesto over the pasta and toss well. Serve warm.

romaine salad with shiitake mushrooms & garlic ▶

SERVES:
4 to 8

This gorgeous, full-flavored, and sturdy salad is great for picnics. You can mix the dressing in a little jar and dress the salad when you're ready to eat.

PREPARATION TIME:
20 minutes

COOKING TIME:
14 minutes

STORAGE:
Not suitable for storage.

1 romaine lettuce, washed and dried
2 tbsp. butter
10 to 12 garlic cloves, cut lengthwise into slivers
3 cups shiitake mushrooms brushed clean, stems discarded, and caps cut into ½in.-thick slices
3 tbsp. olive oil
1 tbsp. balsamic vinegar
2 tbsp. shaved Parmesan cheese
salt

1 Reserve the smaller middle leaves from the lettuce and chop the remaining leaves in ½-inch-wide strips. Put them in a large salad bowl and set aside.

2 Heat a large skillet over medium-high heat. Add the butter and garlic and cook 4 minutes, stirring occasionally, until it is starting to brown. Add the mushrooms and continue cooking 10 minutes longer, stirring continuously, until brown and crisp. Remove from the heat and leave to cool.

3 Add the mushroom mixture to the chopped lettuce and sprinkle with the olive oil, balsamic vinegar, and Parmesan. Season with salt and toss well. Spoon the salad into the reserved lettuce leaves and serve.

lemon–cinnamon apple slices

SERVES:
8

Fresh fruit is a must on a picnic, and these refreshing, ready-to-eat slices are great for little hands.

PREPARATION TIME:
10 minutes

STORAGE:
Refrigerate up to 1 day.

3 apples, halved, cored, and cut into wedges
juice of ½ lemon
½ tsp. cinnamon

1 Put the apples in a medium bowl. Sprinkle with the lemon juice and toss until well coated.

2 Sprinkle the cinnamon over the apples and toss until well coated. Serve either before or after the meal.

cinnamon
comes from the bark of the cinnamon tree and is one of the oldest known spices. A great source of manganese, iron, and calcium, it's also a natural food preservative, inhibiting bacteria and preventing spoiling.

spelt pasta with pesto

SERVES:
1

PREPARATION
TIME:
5 minutes

COOKING TIME:
10 minutes

Warm a thermos with boiling water before packing this easy dish, and by lunchtime your child will have delicious, still-warm pasta to savor.

½ cup dried wholegrain
  spelt penne
2 tbsp. basil pesto
  (see page 154)
salt

1 Bring a small saucepan of salted water to a boil over high heat and cook the pasta according to the package directions. Meanwhile, fill a small thermos with boiling water and set aside.

2 Drain the pasta, then return it to the pan and mix in the pesto.

3 Drain the hot water from the thermos and transfer the pasta into the thermos. Don't forget to pack a fork!

corn pasta with tomato sauce

SERVES:
1

PREPARATION
TIME:
5 minutes

COOKING TIME:
10 minutes

Corn pasta adds a different grain into your lunchbox rota. This dish is a great opportunity to use some of the homemade tomato sauce you've been keeping in the freezer – simply defrost it in the fridge the night before or in a pan over a medium heat while the pasta cooks.

salt
¾ cup corn spirelli
2 tbsp. tomato sauce
  (see page 117)

1 Bring a small saucepan of salted water to a boil over high heat and cook the pasta according to the package directions. Meanwhile, fill a thermos with boiling water and set aside.

2 Drain the pasta, then return it to the pan. Add the tomato sauce and mix well.

3 Drain the hot water from the thermos and transfer the pasta into the thermos.

▲ cheddar & watercress sandwich

Sharp cheddar is wonderfully flavorful. Nicholas loves it matched with the mustard, mayonnaise, and watercress in this recipe.

SERVES:
1

PREPARATION TIME:
10 minutes

1 slice of wholewheat bread
non-hot mustard, for spreading
mayonnaise, for spreading
1oz. sharp cheddar cheese, sliced
2 or 3 watercress sprigs

1 If the bread is fresh, use it as is. If it is frozen, make the sandwich with frozen bread—it will thaw and be soft by the time your child is ready for lunch. Cut the bread in half and spread one half with mustard and the other with mayo.

2 Put the cheese on one half of the bread, then top with the watercress and cover with the other half of the bread.

3 Wrap the sandwich in waxed paper, put it in a little plastic bag, and seal to keep it fresh. Have your child bring the plastic bag back home so you can re-use it many times, washing it out as necessary.

hemp seed & egg salad sandwich

SERVES:
1

PREPARATION TIME:
10 minutes

COOKING TIME:
9 minutes

Hemp seeds have a subtle, nutty flavor, so your child might not even taste them—but they add excellent nutrition to a lovely sandwich.

1 egg, at room temperature
1 tbsp. mayonnaise, plus extra for spreading
1 tsp. shelled hemp seeds
1 slice of wholegrain rye bread

1 Pierce the large end of the egg with a pin. Bring a small saucepan of water to a boil and, using a spoon, carefully put the eggs in the water. Boil 9 minutes, then remove from the heat, drain the hot water from the pan, and refill it with cold water to cool the egg and stop it cooking. Leave to cool 5 minutes.

2 Peel the egg and put it in a small bowl. Add the mayonnaise and mash with a fork. Add the hemp seeds and mix well.

3 Cut the bread in half and spread with mayonnaise. Spoon the egg salad onto one half of the bread (you will have some left over) and then cover with the other half of the bread. Wrap the sandwich in waxed paper and then put in a little plastic bag and seal to keep it fresh. Have your child bring the plastic bag back home so you can re-use it many times, washing it out as necessary.

arugula & lemon salad

SERVES:
1

PREPARATION TIME:
5 minutes

Arugula with lemon juice is divine—and because you're not adding olive oil, the leaves are still fresh and crisp at lunchtime.

1 handful arugula leaves, roughly chopped
1 lemon wedge

1 Put the arugula in a small container and squeeze the lemon over.

2 Mix well and seal the container.

arugula
and other bitter salad greens are an excellent source of antioxidants. Arugula is also packed with vitamin C, which is important for healthy teeth and gums and for fighting infection; and calcium, which is needed for strong bones.

carrot & pea salad

Jessie loves this colorful salad. It's lovely and fresh, and the balsamic vinegar gives it a gentle sweetness. The frozen peas will defrost by lunchtime and will really brighten up your child's meal.

SERVES:
1

PREPARATION
TIME:
5 minutes

1 small carrot, grated
2 tbsp. frozen peas
1 tsp. balsamic vinegar

1 Put the carrot, peas (leave frozen), and vinegar in a bowl and mix well.

2 Transfer to a small container and seal. By the time your child is ready for lunch the peas will be defrosted.

cucumber & tomato salad

Crunchy and refreshing, this salad will liven up your child's lunchbox. Cucumber and tomato are a great duo, and the mayonnaise adds a delightful creaminess.

SERVES:
1

PREPARATION
TIME:
10 minutes

2in. piece cucumber,
quartered lengthwise,
then quartered
crosswise
4 cherry tomatoes,
quartered
1 tbsp. mayonnaise

1 Put the cucumber, tomato, and mayonnaise in a bowl and mix well.

2 Transfer to a small container and seal.

cucumber
packs a nutritional
punch. Among other
nutrients, it provides silica,
which helps to strengthen
connective tissue. It also has
folate and vitamins A and C.
Organic cucumbers have
higher levels of vitamin
C than conventional
ones.

chickpea pancakes

Finger foods are great at parties, and these are perfect for little fingers. They have a nice flavor without being too strong.

MAKES:
12 pancakes

PREPARATION TIME:
10 minutes, plus overnight soaking

COOKING TIME:
2 hours 25 minutes

STORAGE:
Refrigerate the cooked pancakes up to 3 days.

½ cup dried chickpeas
2 tsp. lemon juice
1 strip of kombu, about 3¼ x 2in.
wholewheat flour
   wholegrain spelt flour, as needed (optional)
1 tsp. ground cumin
½ tsp. salt

1 Put the chickpeas and lemon juice in a medium saucepan, cover with warm water, and leave to soak, covered, overnight.

2 Drain and rinse the chickpeas. Return them to the pan and add 2 cups water. Bring to a boil over high heat and boil 10 minutes, skimming any scum that rises to the surface. Add the kombu, reduce the heat to low, and cook, covered, 2 hours, or until tender. Remove from the heat and drain. If using a blender with a plastic container, leave the chickpeas and kombu to cool completely before blending.

3 Transfer the chickpeas and kombu to a blender and blend 1 minute, or until smooth, adding just enough fresh water to form a thick batter. If you add too much water and the mixture is runny, add a little flour, 1 tablespoon at a time, until it thickens. Transfer the mixture to a bowl and stir in the cumin and salt.

4 Heat a griddle over medium heat. Working in batches, if necessary, drop teaspoonfuls of the chickpea batter onto the griddle. They will spread a little and should be about 1¼ inches in diameter. Cook 2 to 3 minutes until bubbles pop through the surface and the underside of the pancakes is light brown. Flip over and cook 2 to 3 minutes longer until light brown. Serve hot or warm.

chickpeas are high in fiber, which helps to avoid rapid rises in blood sugar levels after eating. Combined with grains, they are a fat-free protein, so serve them with good oils, such as hemp seed or flaxseed oil, for a well-rounded, healthy meal.

sesame & raisin bread balls

With their little sweet raisin bits inside, these are great for parties, especially warm from the oven. They also help fill up little tummies.

MAKES:
40 to 45 balls

PREPARATION TIME:
30 minutes, plus 3½ hours rising

COOKING TIME:
35 minutes

STORAGE:
Store the baked bread balls in an airtight container up to 2 days. The dough can be made to the end of step 1 and refrigerated up to 3 days. Punch it down once a day and re-cover, or freeze up to 3 months in a plastic bag, squeezing out any excess air. To bake, leave the dough to come to room temperature and double in size, then continue from step 3.

raisins
are excellent for relieving constipation and reducing acidity. They're antiviral and antibacterial, too. Raisins are packed with iron and aid bone and teeth health and vision.

1 tsp. olive oil, plus extra for greasing and coating the dough
2½ cups wholegrain spelt flour
1½ tsp. active dry yeast
1½ tsp. salt
1½ tsp. kefir or plain yogurt
butter, for greasing
2 tbsp. sesame seeds
¼ cup raisins, coarsely chopped

1 Grease a medium bowl with olive oil and set aside. In a large bowl, mix together the flour, yeast, and salt. Add the olive oil, kefir, and ¾ cup lukewarm water. Mix with your hands until it nearly comes together, adding an additional 1 to 2 tablespoons water, if necessary. Tip the contents of the bowl onto the work surface and knead by stretching the dough away from you, then gathering it back, turning it 90 degrees, and repeating, incorporating all of the flour as you knead. The dough might seem a little dry at first, but the ingredients will come together as you work. Knead 10 minutes, or until smooth and elastic. If the dough is sticking to your hands, add a little more flour a bit at a time; if it is too dry for the dry ingredients to come together, add a little more water.

2 Transfer the dough to the oiled bowl, rubbing a little olive oil over the surface of the dough. Put a clean, damp dish towel on the surface of the dough so it doesn't dry out and form a crust, and leave to rise at room temperature 1½ to 2 hours until double in size.

3 Grease a cookie sheet with butter and set aside. Turn the dough out onto the countertop and punch down. Knead 1 minute, then shape it into a ball and transfer to the cookie sheet. Cover with the damp dish towel and leave to rise at room temperature 1 to 1½ hours until double in size.

4 Preheat the oven to 425°F. Put the sesame seeds in a shallow bowl and set aside. Punch down the dough again and flatten it with your hand, then pour the raisins on top and knead them into the dough until incorporated. Pull off small pieces of the dough and roll them into 1-inch balls, pinching the dough around any raisins that are sticking out. Roll the dough balls in the sesame seeds and put them on a cookie sheet. Working in batches, bake 15 to 18 minutes until light brown. Cool on a wire rack for a few minutes before serving warm.

mini pita pizzas

It's hard to go wrong with pizza—for parties or any other time.

MAKES:
8 pizzas

PREPARATION TIME:
10 minutes

COOKING TIME:
5 minutes

STORAGE:
Not suitable for storage.

4 mini wholewheat pita breads
⅓ cup crumbled goat cheese
4 tbsp. tomato sauce (see page 117)
⅓ cup diced mozzarella cheese
¼–½ tsp. dried oregano

BASIL PESTO
2 tbsp. pine nuts
1 cup tightly packed basil leaves
1 garlic clove, chopped
4 tbsp. grated Parmesan cheese
2 tbsp. olive oil
¼ tsp. salt

1 Preheat the broiler to medium. Put the pine nuts for the pesto in a pan and heat over medium-low heat, stirring continuously, until lightly toasted, then set aside to cool. Put the pita breads on a baking sheet and lightly toast under the broiler until they puff up and are lightly browned. Carefully cut them in half by slicing around the edge of each pita with a sharp knife to produce 2 circles from each pitta.

2 To make the pesto, put the pine nuts, basil, garlic, Parmesan, olive oil and salt in a food processor and process for 1–2 minutes until the mixture forms a thick paste. Spread 1 teaspoon of the pesto over 4 of the pitta circles, then crumble the goat cheese over the pesto. Spread 1 tablespoon of the tomato sauce over each of the remaining 4 pita circles and divide the mozzarella over the sauce. Put the pitas on the baking sheet, sprinkle sparingly with the oregano and grill for 2 minutes until crunchy and the cheese has melted. Serve hot.

cherry tomatoes with hummus & capers

Most kids love tomatoes, especially sweet cherry tomatoes. These pretty bite-size morsels can be popped into little mouths one at a time.

MAKES:
30

PREPARATION TIME:
20 minutes, plus making the hummus

STORAGE:
Not suitable for storage.

30 cherry tomatoes
1 recipe quantity hummus (see page 97)
2 tbsp. small capers or 30 large caper berries

1 Cut off the tops of the tomatoes and, using a melon baller or small spoon, scoop the middle and seeds out of the tomatoes, and discard.

2 Fill the tomatoes with the hummus, using a tiny spoon. Top each tomato with 4 or 5 tiny capers or 1 caper berry, then serve.

▼ sweet potato & carrot patties

These delicious patties are always a hit at parties. You'll want to make them ahead of time and keep them warm in a low oven.

MAKES:
12 patties

PREPARATION TIME:
15 minutes

COOKING TIME:
30 minutes

STORAGE:
Refrigerate the cooked patties up to 3 days.

3 cups diced sweet
   potatoes
8oz. carrots, cut
   into thin rounds
1 tbsp. sesame seeds
3 or 4 scallions, trimmed
   and sliced into circles
wholegrain spelt flour,
   for coating (optional)
4 tbsp. Greek-style yogurt
½ tsp. curry powder
sliced cucumber, to serve

1 Put the sweet potatoes and carrots in a steamer and steam, covered, over boiling water 20 minutes, or until soft. Meanwhile, put the sesame seeds in a medium saucepan and heat over medium-low heat 3 to 4 minutes, shaking the pan occasionally, until the seeds begin to brown and just start popping. Set aside.

2 Preheat the broiler to medium. Put the sweet potatoes and carrots in a bowl and mash with a fork, then mix in the sesame seeds and scallions. Shape the mixture into 12 balls of equal size, then flatten into 2½-inch patties about ¾ inch high. If they are very sticky, sprinkle both sides with flour. Put the patties on a cookie sheet. Broil 5 minutes on each side, or until warm through and light brown.

3 Meanwhile, put the yogurt and curry powder in a small bowl and mix well. Serve the patties warm with the sauce and sliced cucumbers.

cheesy polenta bites

MAKES:
80 bites

PREPARATION
TIME:
10 minutes

COOKING TIME:
20 minutes

STORAGE:
Refrigerate
up to 3 days.

Nicholas always goes back for more and more of this simply irresistible finger food. Corn makes a nice addition at a party, and kids love the delicious melted cheese.

butter, for greasing
1½ tsp. salt
1 cup cornmeal
¾ cup coarsely grated
  Parmesan cheese
2 tbsp. finely grated
  Parmesan cheese

1 Preheat the broiler to medium and grease the bottom of a 10-inch square baking pan with butter. In a heavy-bottomed saucepan, bring 3¾ cups water to a boil over high heat. Add the salt and then the cornmeal, whisking vigorously to avoid lumps before it begins to thicken. Reduce the heat to medium-low and cook 15 minutes, stirring continuously with a wooden spoon, or until thick and stiff. Remove from the heat, then mix in the coarsely grated Parmesan cheese.

2 Pour the polenta into the pan. Smooth out the surface using a rubber spatula. Spread from the middle outward, pushing the polenta into the corners. Sprinkle over the finely grated Parmesan.

3 Broil 5 minutes, or until light brown. Leave to cool 10 minutes until set. Cut into 1-inch squares and serve hot, warm, or cold.

tofu squares

MAKES:
24 squares

PREPARATION
TIME:
10 minutes, plus
at least 1 hour
marinating

COOKING TIME:
10 minutes

STORAGE:
Refrigerate
up to 3 days.

Herbivores and carnivores alike will love these highly flavored, bite-size squares of tofu. Tofu absorbs the flavors it's cooked with, and the tamari and garlic here really add pizzazz.

4 tbsp. tamari
2 garlic cloves, finely
  chopped
13oz. firm tofu,
  cut into 24 cubes
  of equal size
2 tsp. toasted sesame oil

1 Put the tamari and garlic in a large, shallow dish. Add the tofu and then turn each piece over to coat in the marinade. Cover and chill at least 1 hour, or overnight.

2 Heat the sesame oil in a large skillet over medium-high heat. When it is hot, add the tofu and marinade. Cook 5 minutes on each side, carefully turning the tofu squares over one by one until they are brown, the liquid evaporates, and the garlic is lightly fried. Serve hot or warm.

cream cheese & salmon blinis

MAKES:
50 blinis

If everything is prepared in advance, these are easy to assemble on the day of your party but, if need be, ask someone to help you.

PREPARATION
TIME:
15 minutes

COOKING TIME:
20 minutes

STORAGE:
The cooled blinis can be stored in an airtight container separated by layers of baking parchment. They will keep in the refrigerator up to 3 days.

¼ cup buckwheat flour
¼ cup wholegrain spelt flour
½ tsp. baking powder
⅛ tsp. salt
1 egg
5 tbsp. milk
¼ cup cream cheese
3½oz. smoked salmon, cut into 1in. squares

1 Put the buckwheat flour, spelt flour, baking powder, and salt in a medium bowl and mix well. Add the egg and milk and whisk 1 to 2 minutes until blended.

2 Heat a griddle over medium-low heat. When it is hot, drop teaspoonfuls of the batter onto the griddle, spacing them well apart as they will spread into 2½-inch-wide circles. If the mixture is too thick, add a little more milk. Cook 2 to 3 minutes until bubbles pop on the surface and the underside of the blinis are light brown. Turn them over and cook 2 to 3 minutes longer, or until light brown. Remove from the griddle and leave to cool.

3 Spread a little of the cream cheese on the top of each blini, top with 1 piece of the salmon, and serve.

sweet potato fish balls

MAKES:
36 balls

These unbelievably good fish balls are so quick to make, and they're a great addition to any party-food menu.

PREPARATION
TIME:
15 minutes

COOKING TIME:
25 minutes

STORAGE:
Refrigerate up to 2 days.

2 cups unpeeled sweet potatoes cut into ½in. cubes
8oz. skinned pollock or haddock fillet, roughly chopped (check for bones)
1 egg, beaten
¼ tsp. salt

1 Put the sweet potatoes in a steamer and steam, covered, over boiling water 10 minutes, or until beginning to soften. Add the fish and continue steaming 5 minutes longer, or until the fish is just cooked and the sweet potato is soft.

2 Preheat the broiler to medium-high. Transfer the sweet potato and fish to a bowl and roughly mash with a fork until the mixture comes together but is still chunky. Mix in the egg and salt. The mixture will be a little sticky. Using a large melon baller or two teaspoons, scoop portions of the mixture onto a cookie sheet. Broil 4 to 5 minutes on each side until light brown and warmed through. Serve warm.

spelt cake

SERVES:
12 to 25

PREPARATION
TIME:
35 minutes

COOKING TIME:
50 minutes

STORAGE:
Freeze the baked,
undecorated cake
up to 1 month
or refrigerate
up to 3 days.

This, for me, is the perfect party cake. It's easy to handle, healthy, and delicious. You can decorate it with fruit for the healthiest version or use buttercream frosting, too, for something more decadent.

¾ cup (1½ sticks) butter, plus extra for greasing
1 cup white spelt flour, plus extra for dusting
1 cup rice milk
½ tsp. salt
1½ cups wholegrain spelt flour
1½ tsp. baking powder
5 eggs, at room temperature
2¼ cups sugar
1½ tsp. vanilla extract
50 to 55 red grapes, cut in half or 60 to 65 blueberries (optional)

BUTTERCREAM FROSTING (optional)
3¾ cups powdered sugar
¾ cup (1½ sticks) butter, softened
3 tbsp. milk
1 tsp. vanilla extract
food coloring (optional)

fruit toppings
are delicious, healthy alternatives to sugary frostings. Vitamin-packed grapes and berries can be a great solution to your child's sugar cravings.

1 Preheat the oven to 350°F and grease a 12- x 10-inch cake pan with butter. Line the bottom with baking parchment, then grease and flour. Heat the butter, rice milk, and salt in a small saucepan over low heat until the butter melts and the liquid is hot but not simmering (remove from the heat if necessary).

2 In a medium bowl, sift together the flours and baking powder. In a large bowl, beat the eggs and sugar, using an electric mixer on medium speed, 5 minutes, or until light in colour. Mix in the vanilla extract, then lower the speed to low and beat the flour mixture into the eggs until just blended. Slowly add the hot rice-milk mixture and beat on low speed just until smooth, scraping down the side of the bowl once. Pour the warm batter into the pan.

3 Bake 40 to 45 minutes until the cake begins to pull away from the sides of the pan and a toothpick or skewer inserted in the middle comes out clean. Leave the cake to cool on a wire rack 20 minutes, then slide a knife around the sides of the pan and turn the cake out onto the rack to cool completely.

4 Meanwhile, make the frosting, if using. Put all of the ingredients in a mixing bowl and mix on medium-high speed 10 to 15 minutes until creamed, light, and fluffy, scraping down the sides of the bowl once with a rubber spatula. Stir in the food colouring, if using.

5 If desired, cut the cake into a heart by cutting a heart shape the size of the cake out of a piece of paper. Put the cake, bottom-side up, on a large plate and top with the paper heart. Trace around the heart with a sharp knife, then remove the paper. Holding the knife completely vertically, cut through the tracing lines to make a heart. Set aside the trimmings to snack on later.

6 Spread or pipe the frosting, if using, over the top and sides of the cake. Put the grapes, if using, around the edge. For birthdays, use the remaining grapes to form the number of your child's age in the middle of the cake; otherwise, arrange the remaining grapes on top of the cake. Serve that day.

index